I0474398

Real World

Colouring Book

For Advanced Users & Adults

Copyright 2019 By John Boom

50 Images

Created From Real Life Photos
For You To Colour As You Please.

ISBN 978-0-359-93593-2
90000
9 780359 935932

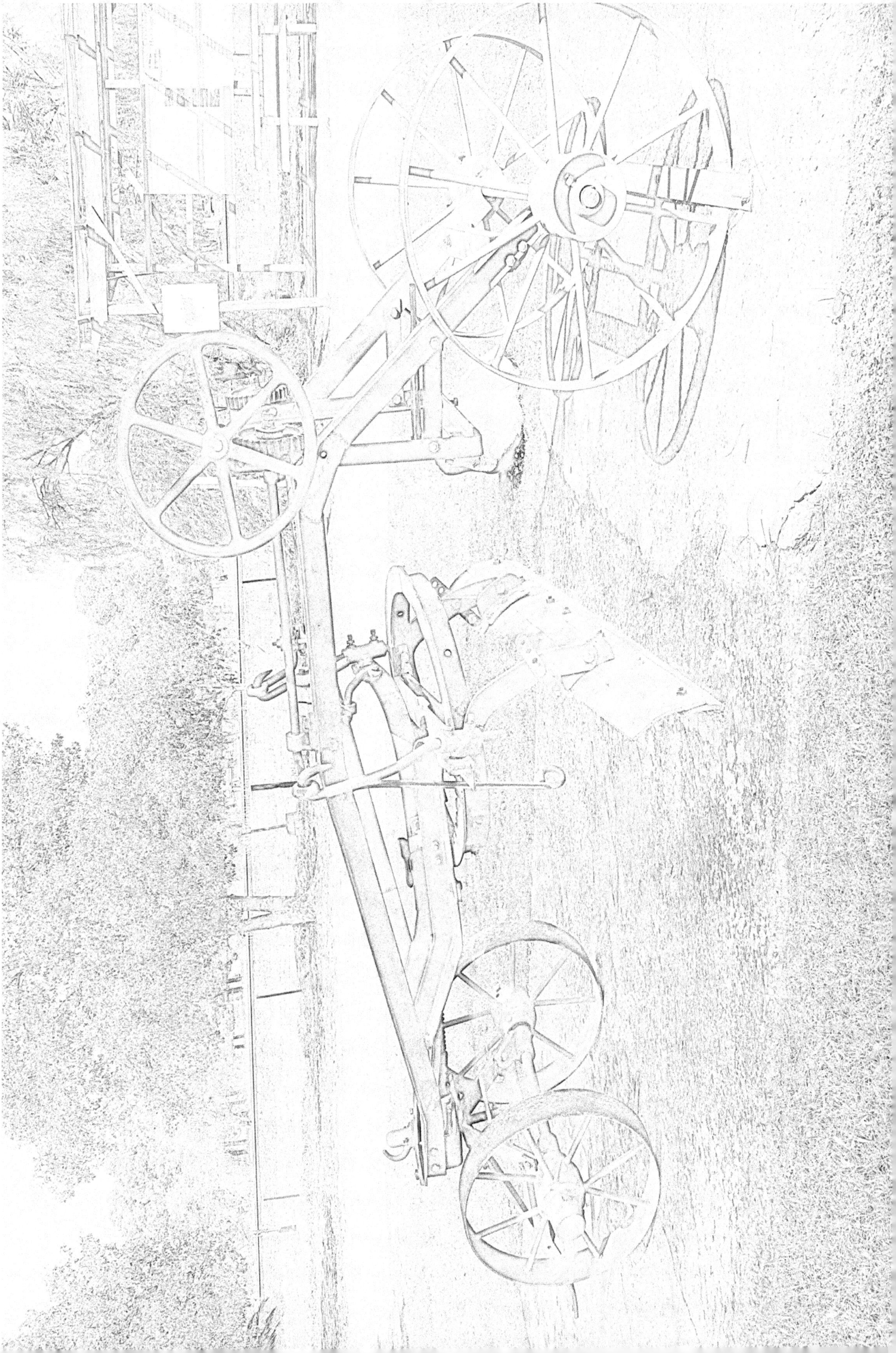

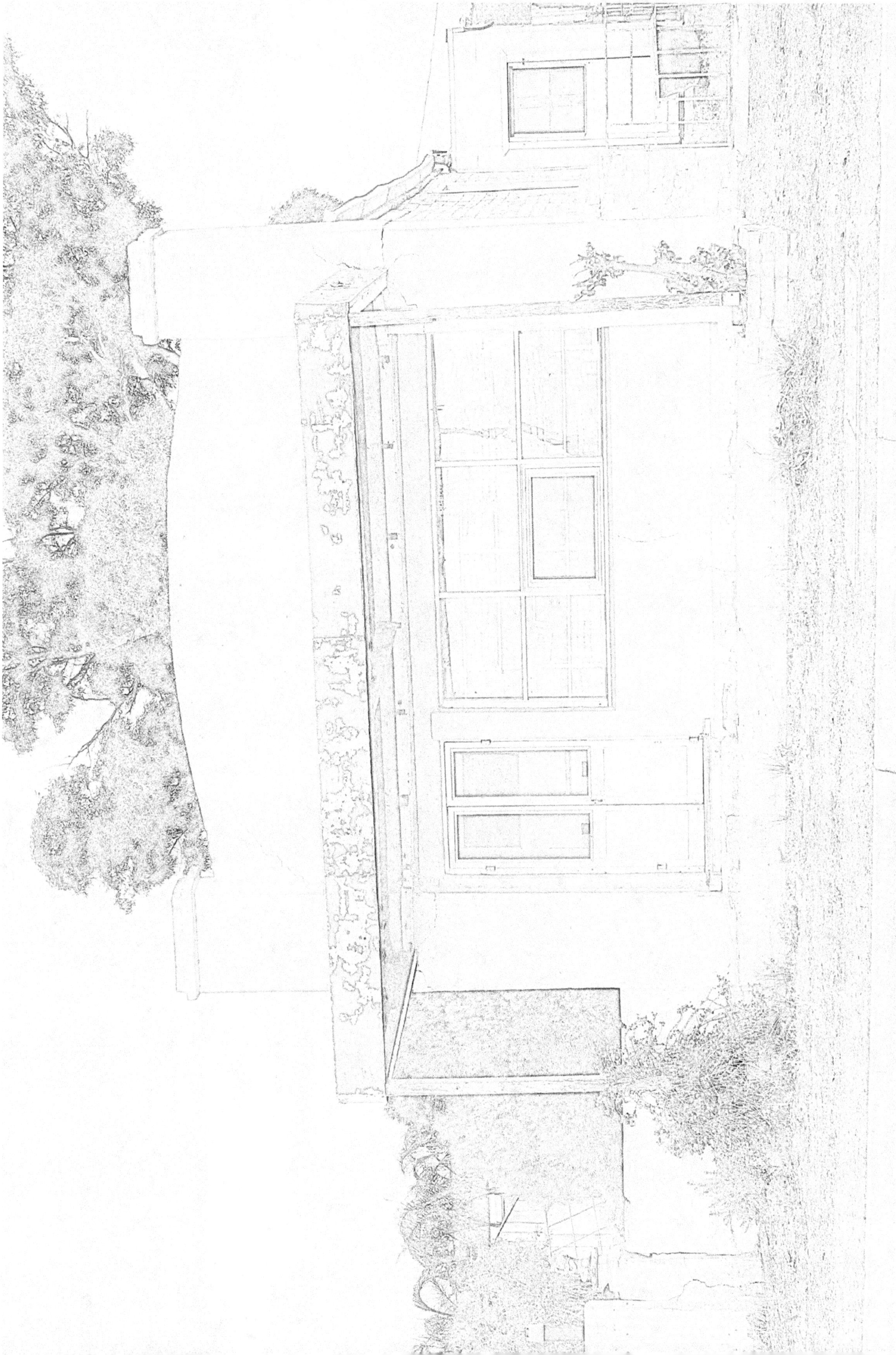

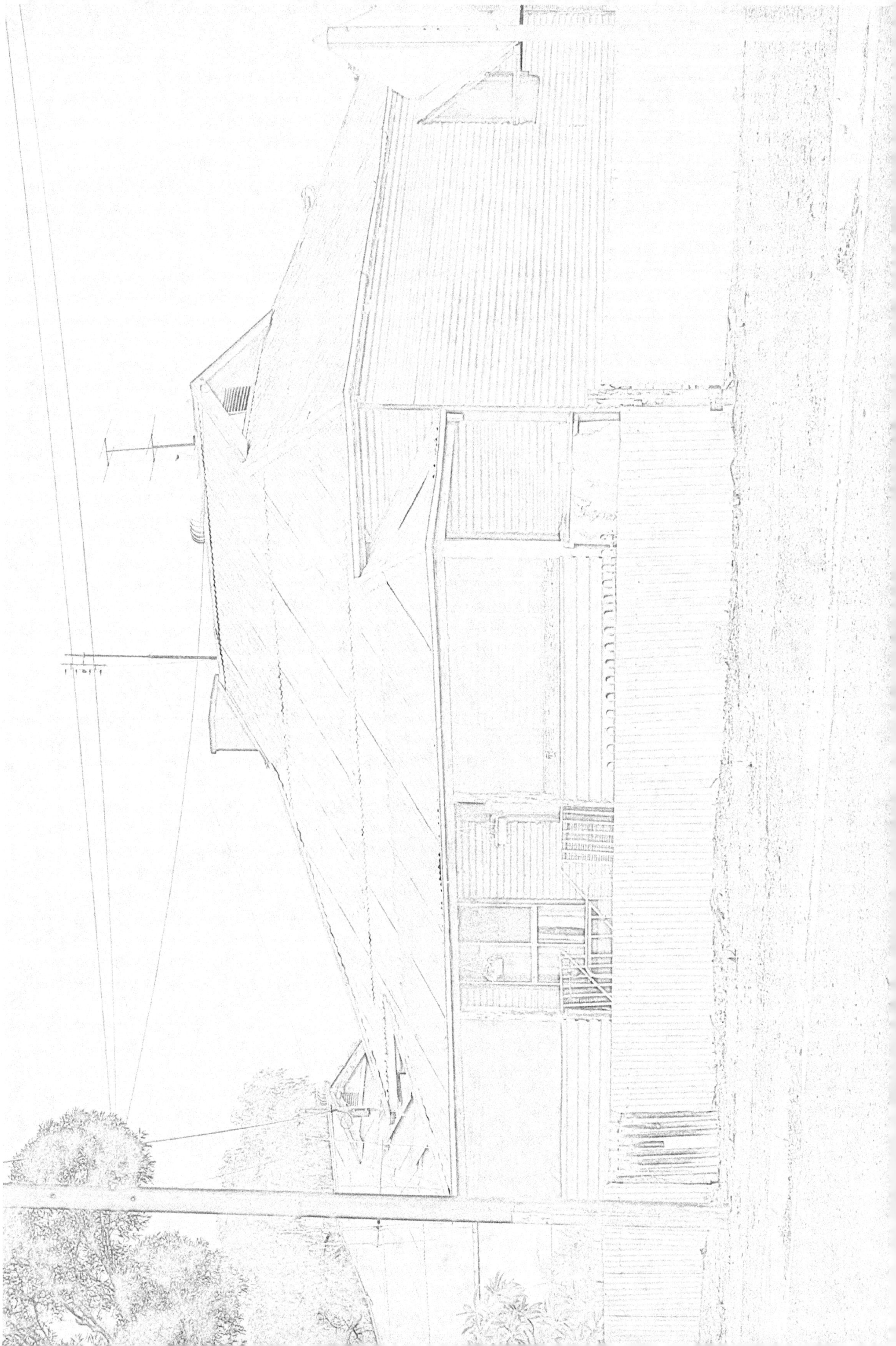

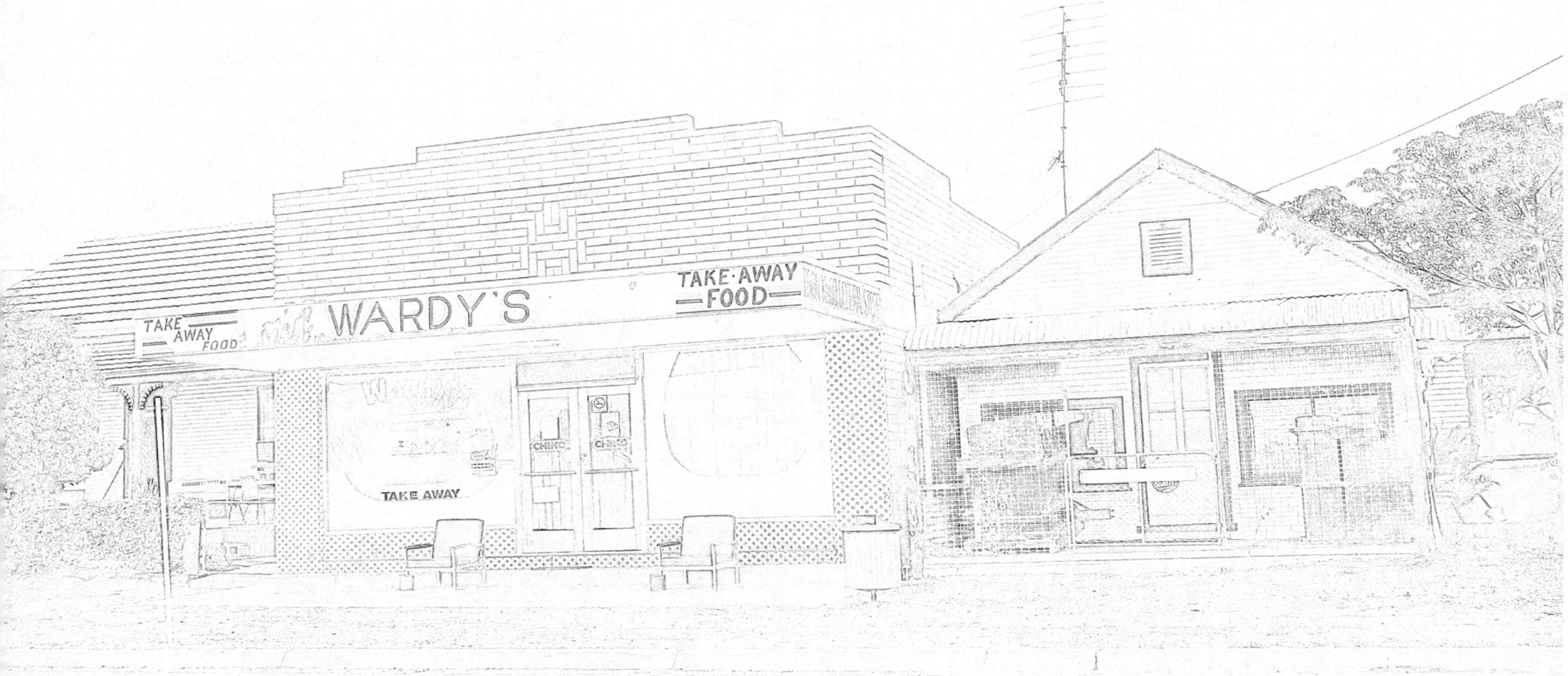
TAKE AWAY FOOD
WARDY'S
TAKE·AWAY FOOD
CHIKO
TAKE AWAY

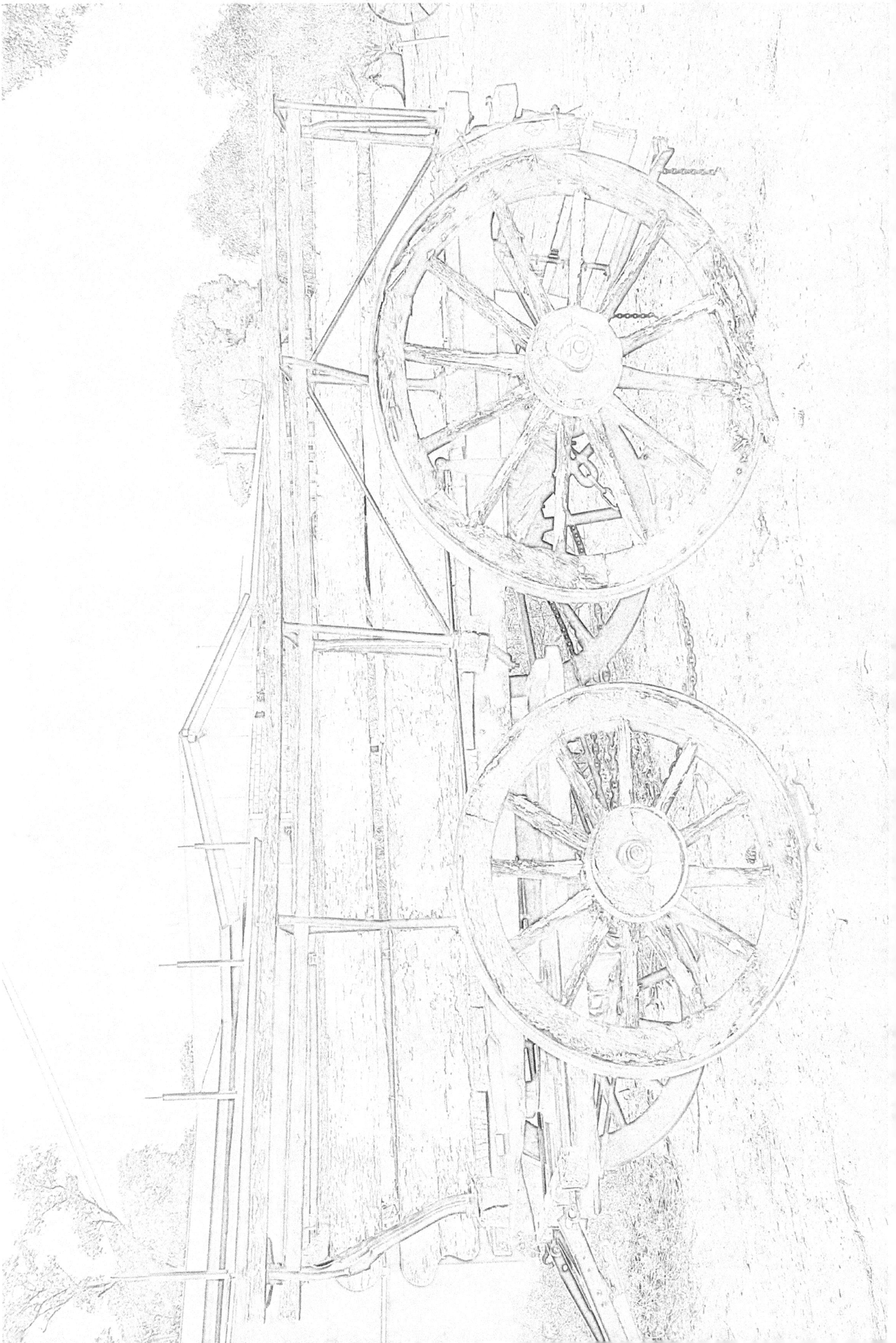

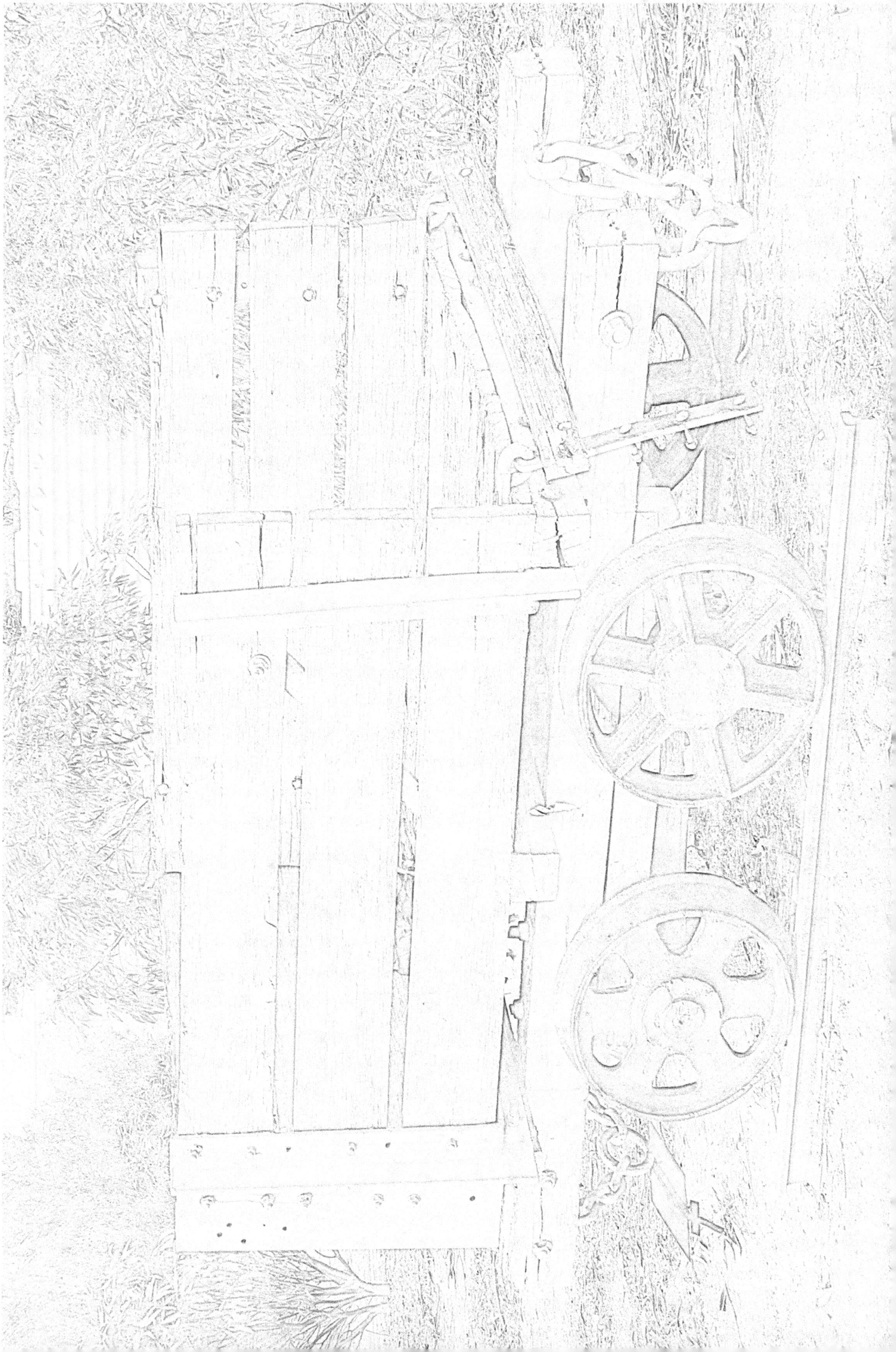

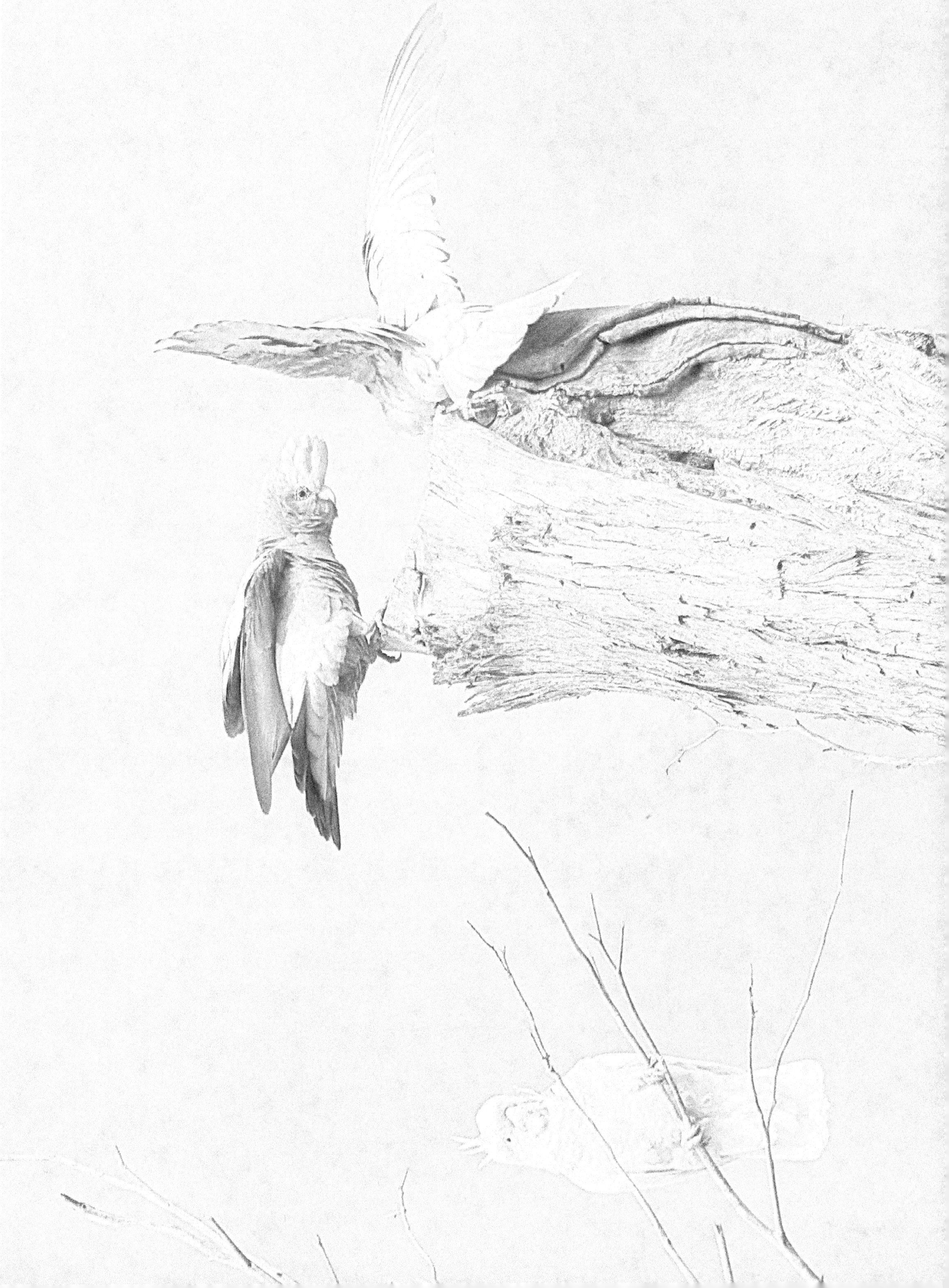

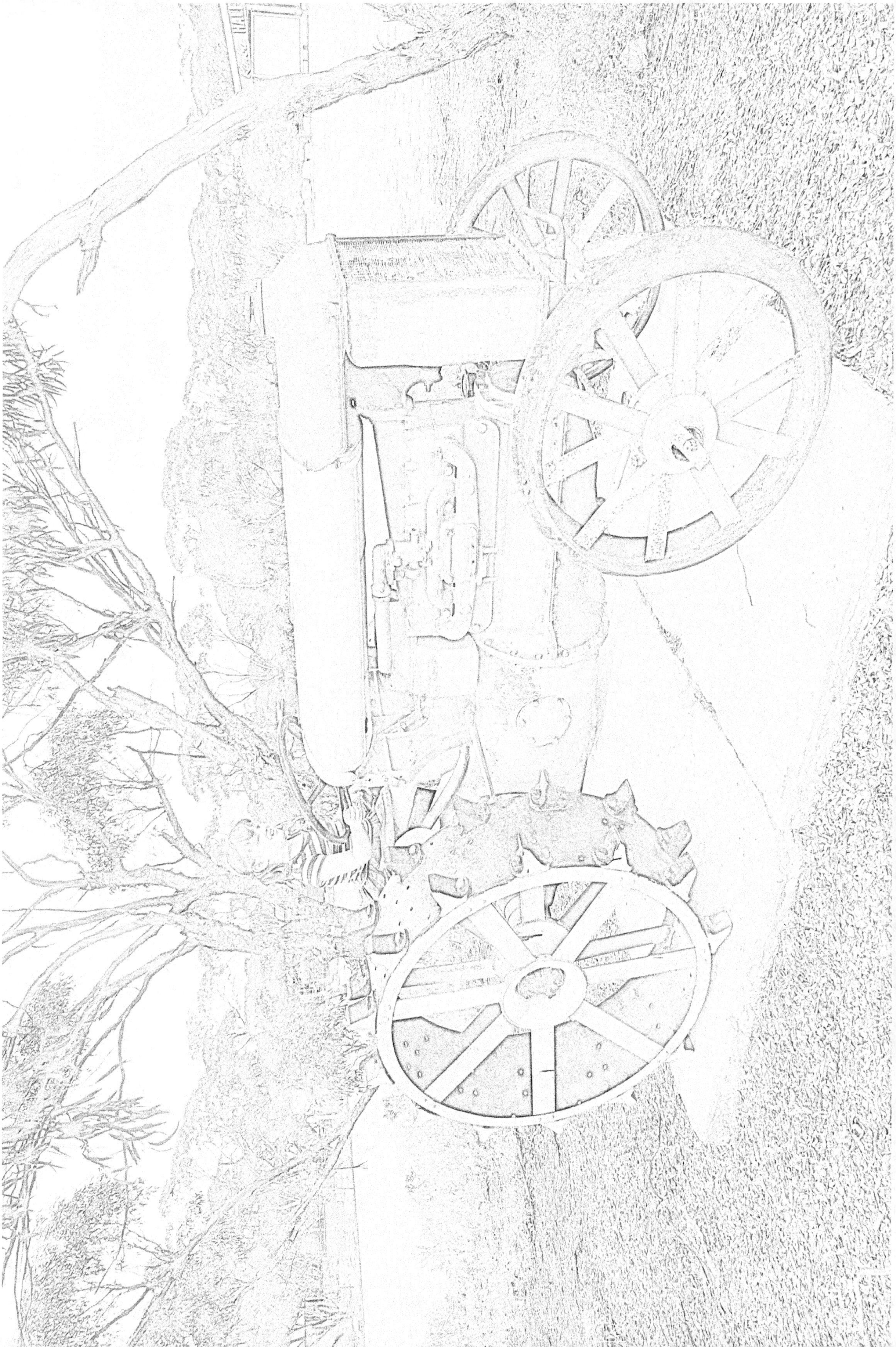

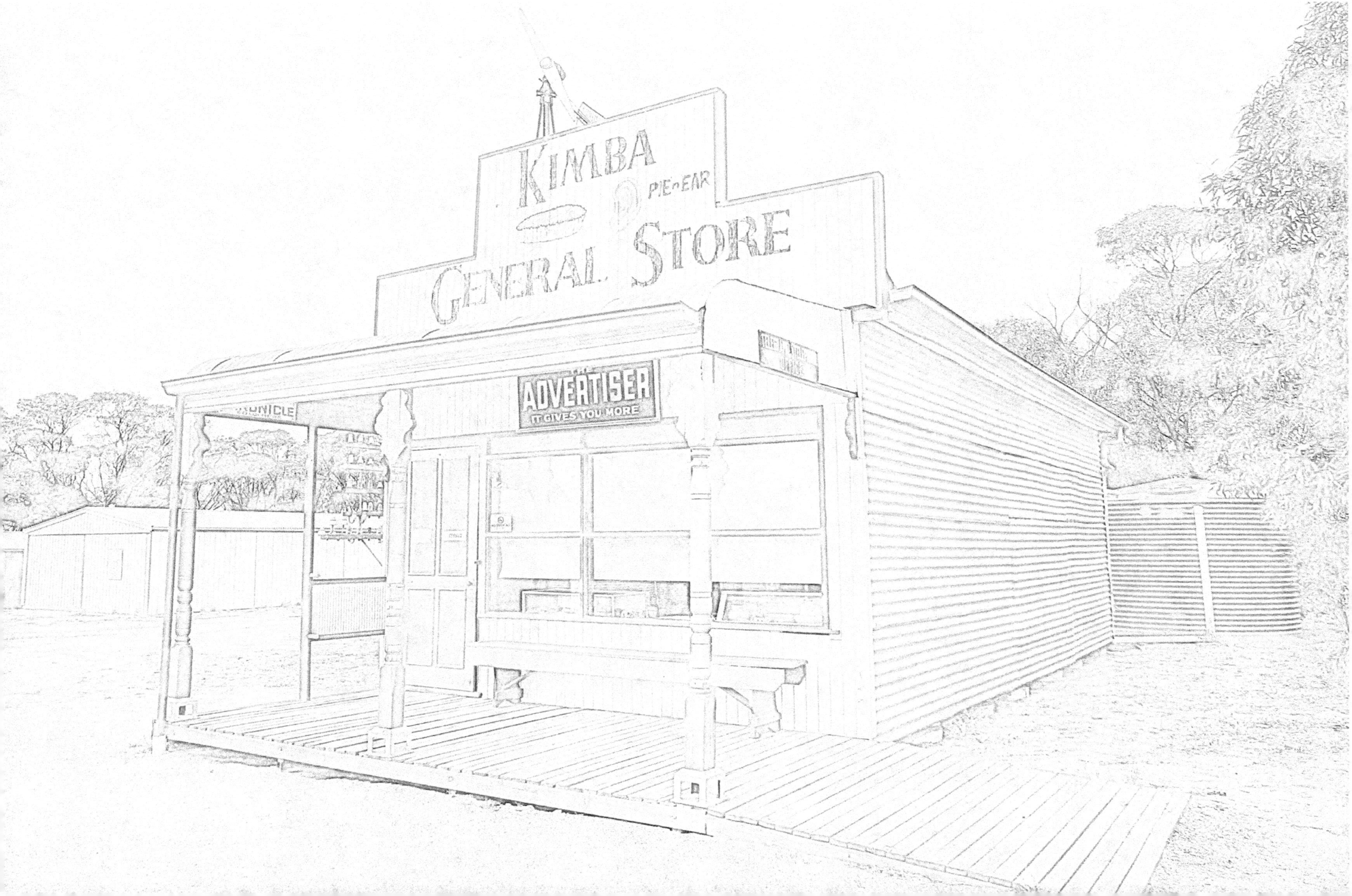
KIMBA
PIE & EAR
GENERAL STORE
ADVERTISER
IT GIVES YOU MORE

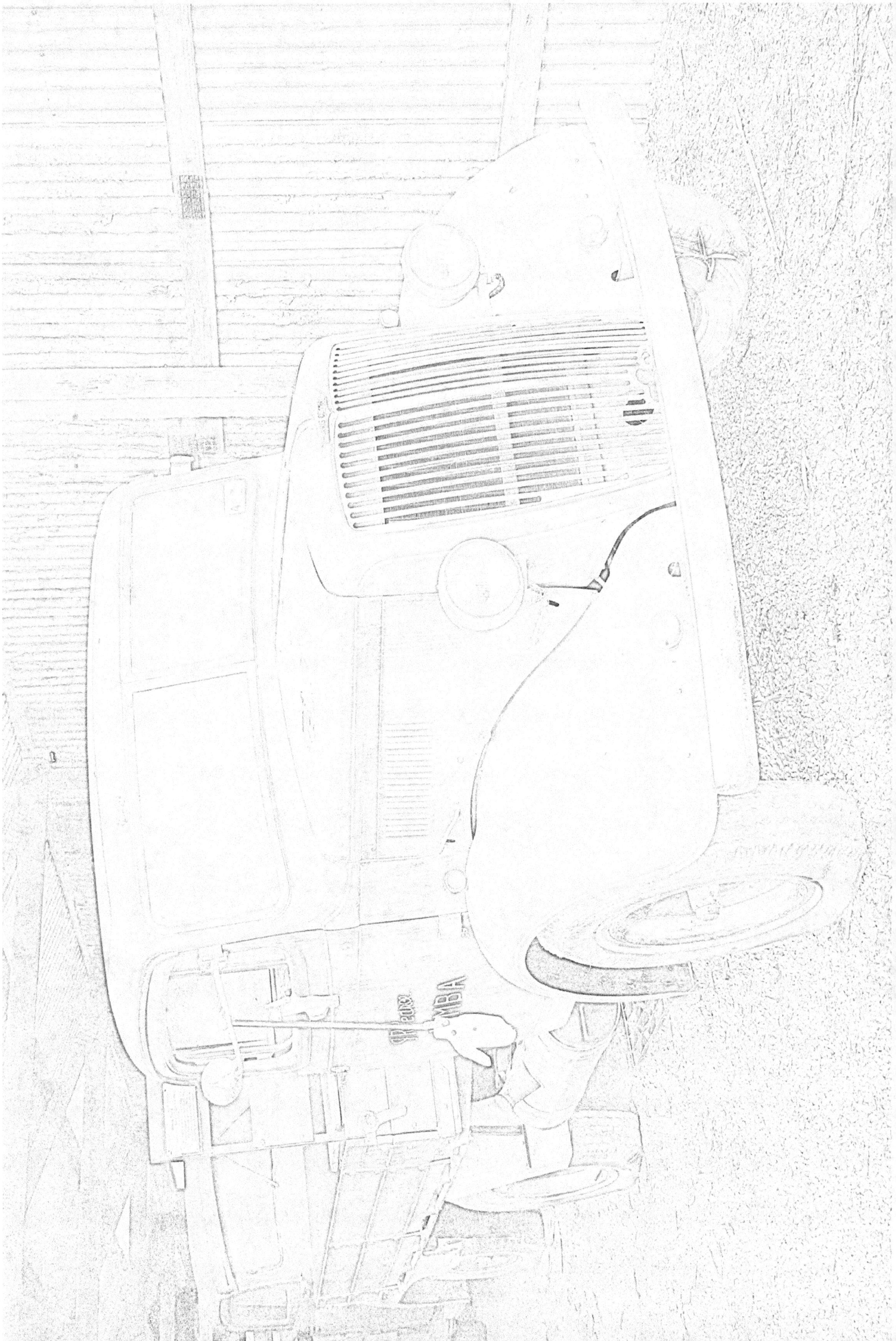

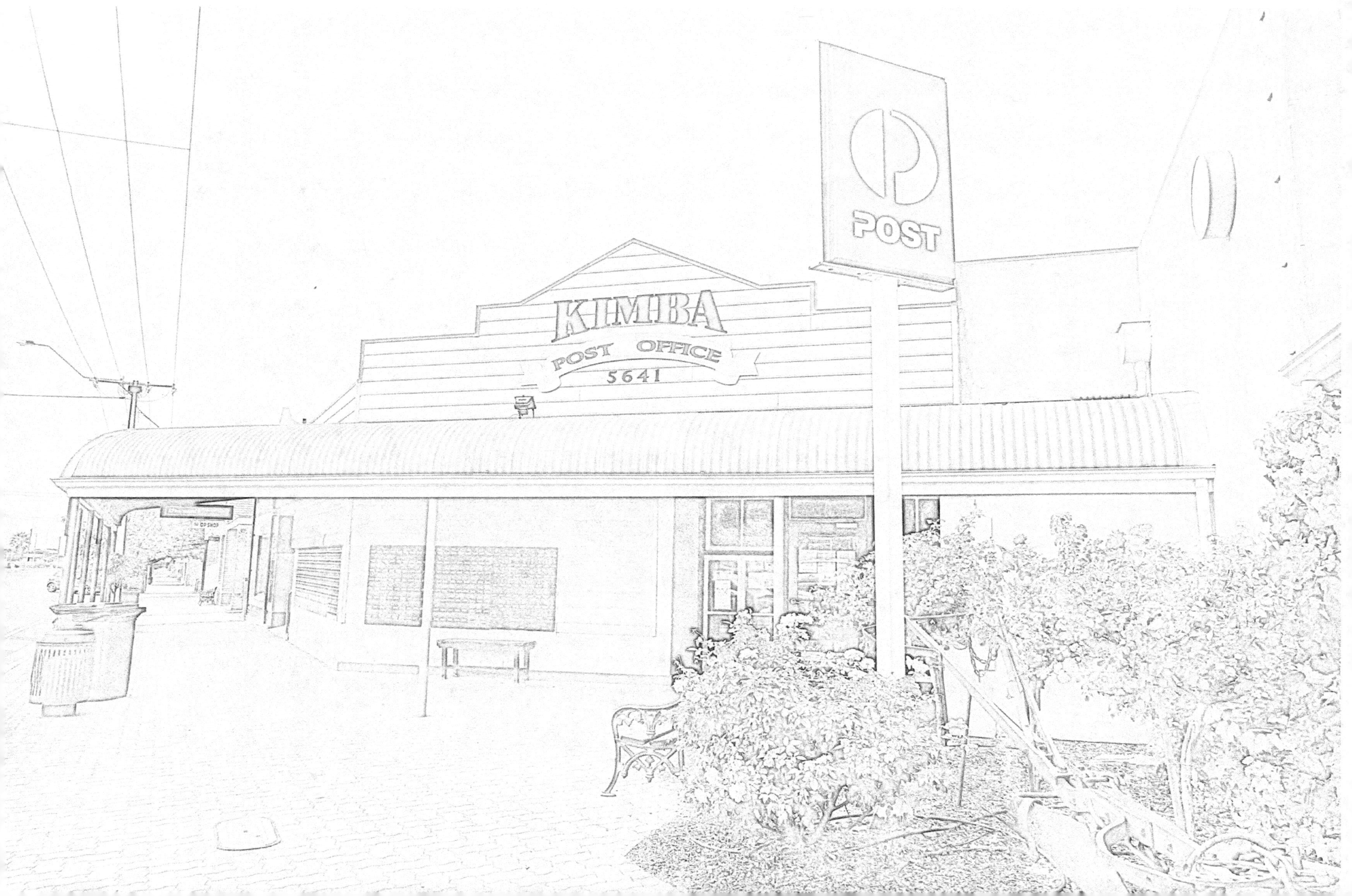
POST
KIMBA
POST OFFICE
5641

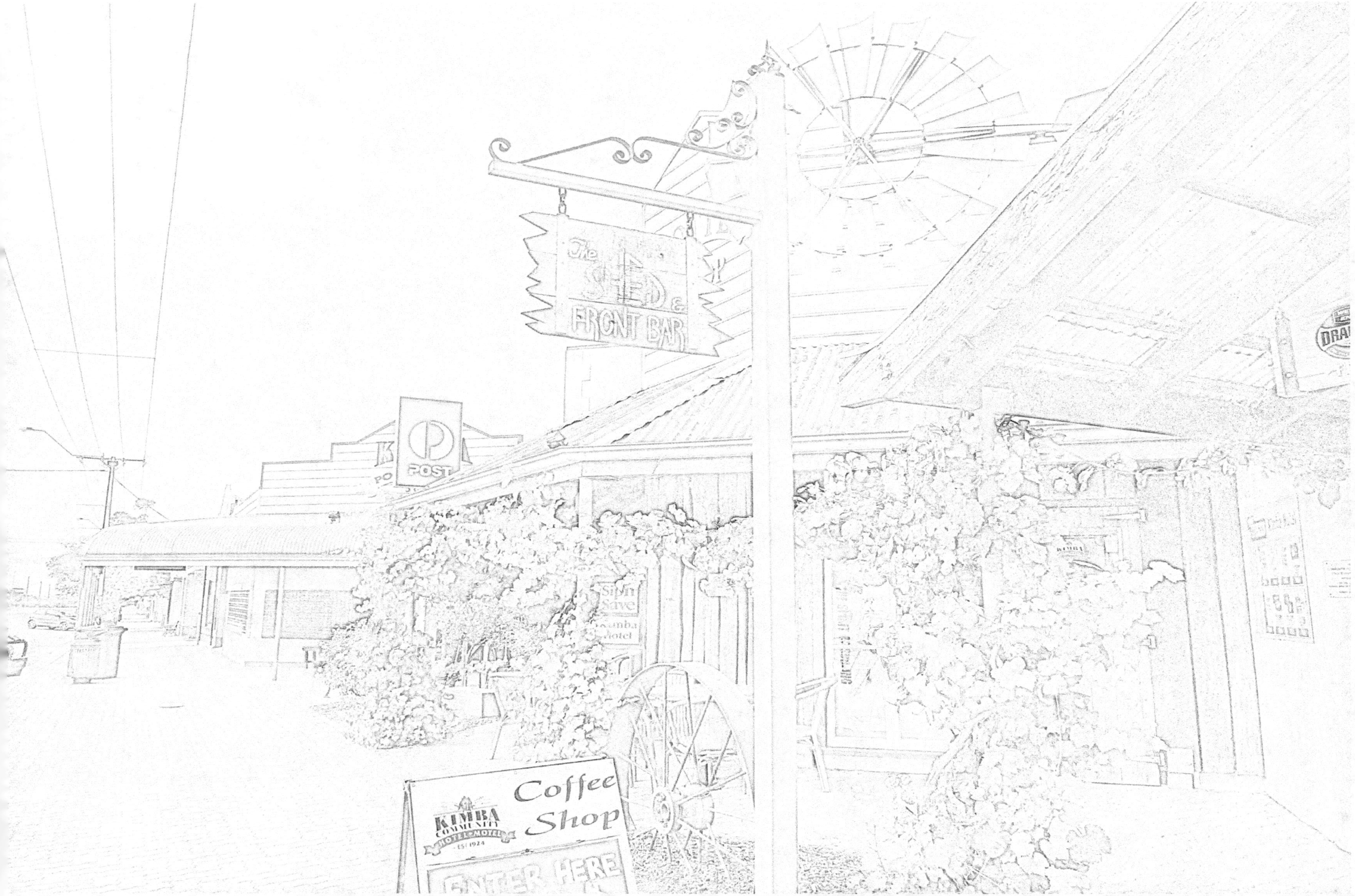
The Shed & Front Bar
POST
Coffee Shop
KIMBA COMMUNITY HOTEL MOTEL
EST 1924
ENTER HERE

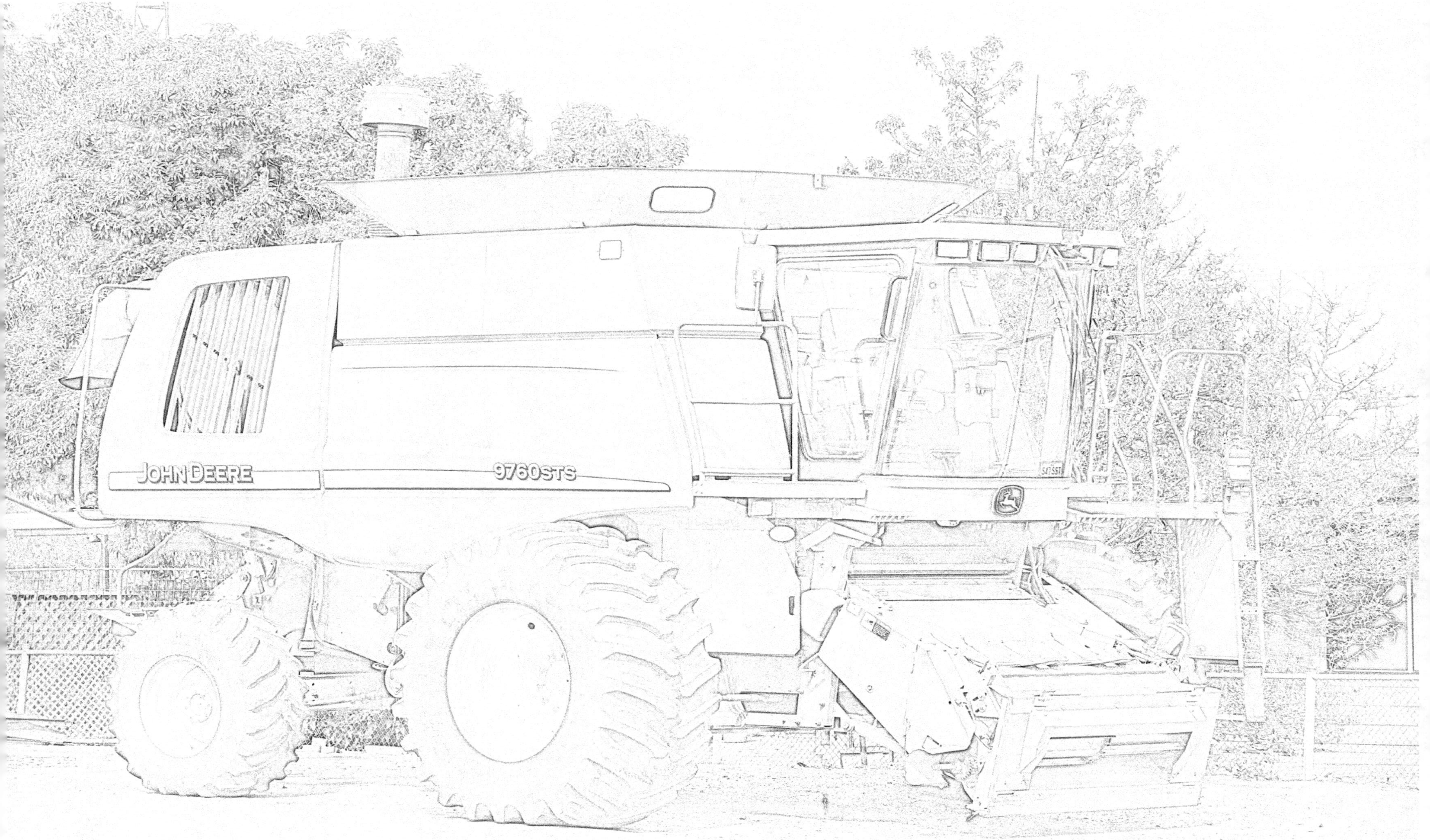
JOHN DEERE
9760STS

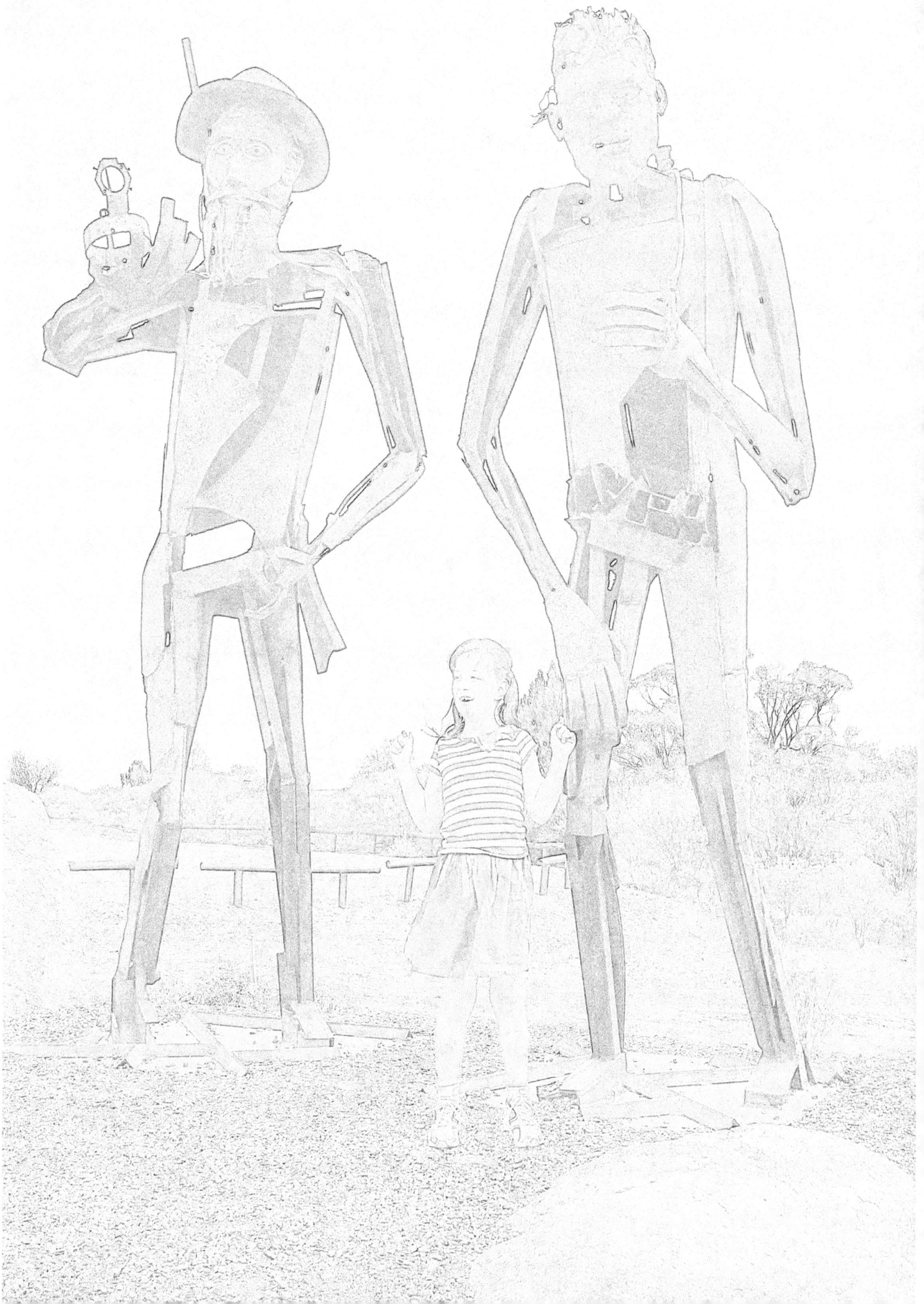

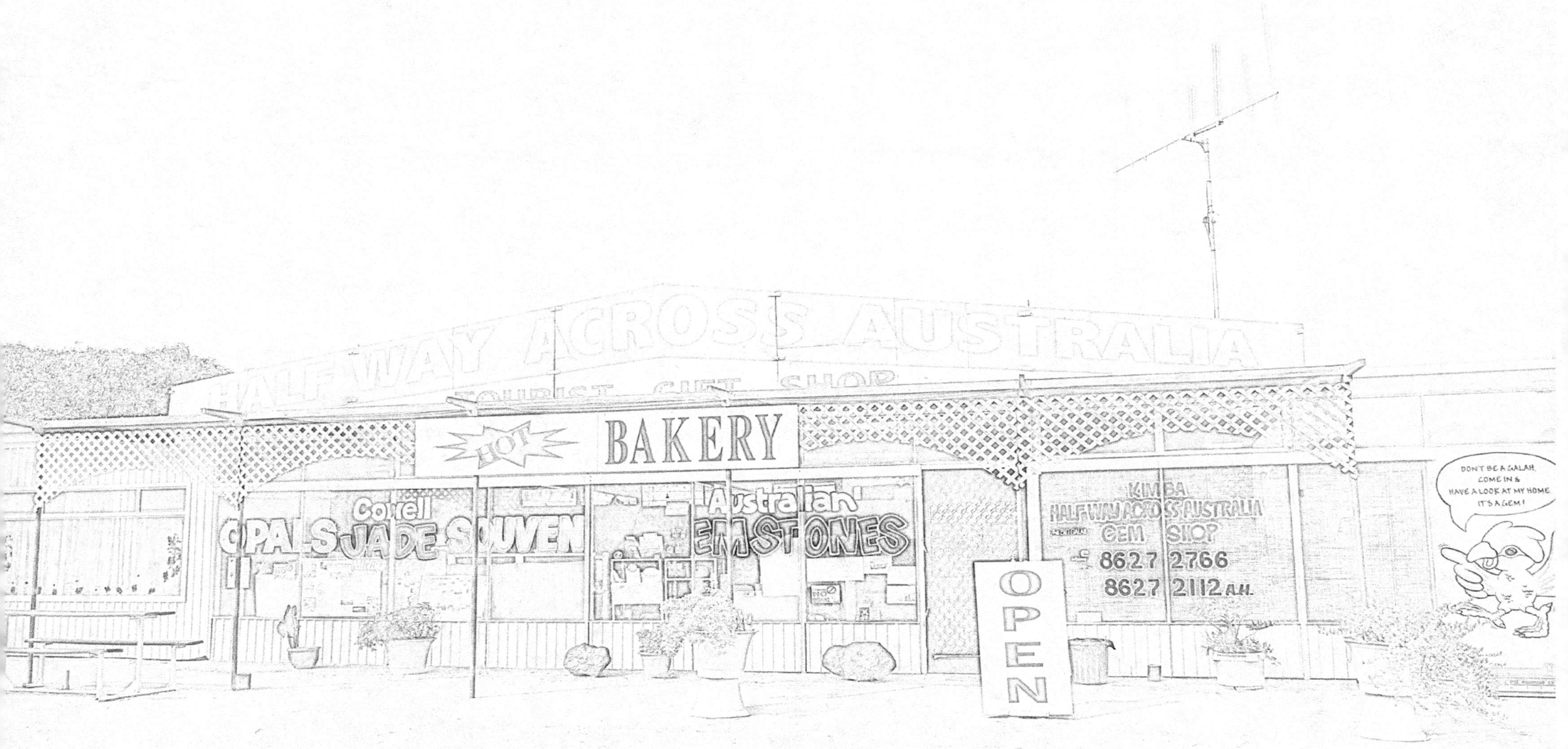
HALF WAY ACROSS AUSTRALIA
TOURIST GIFT SHOP
HOT
BAKERY
Cowell
OPALS JADE SOUVEN
Australian
EMSTONES
KIMBA
HALF WAY ACROSS AUSTRALIA
GEM SHOP
8627 2766
8627 2112 A.H.
OPEN
DON'T BE A GALAH, COME IN & HAVE A LOOK AT MY HOME IT'S A GEM!

LIQUOR BARN
HOTEL MOTEL
The Clock Tower
BOTTLE SHOP

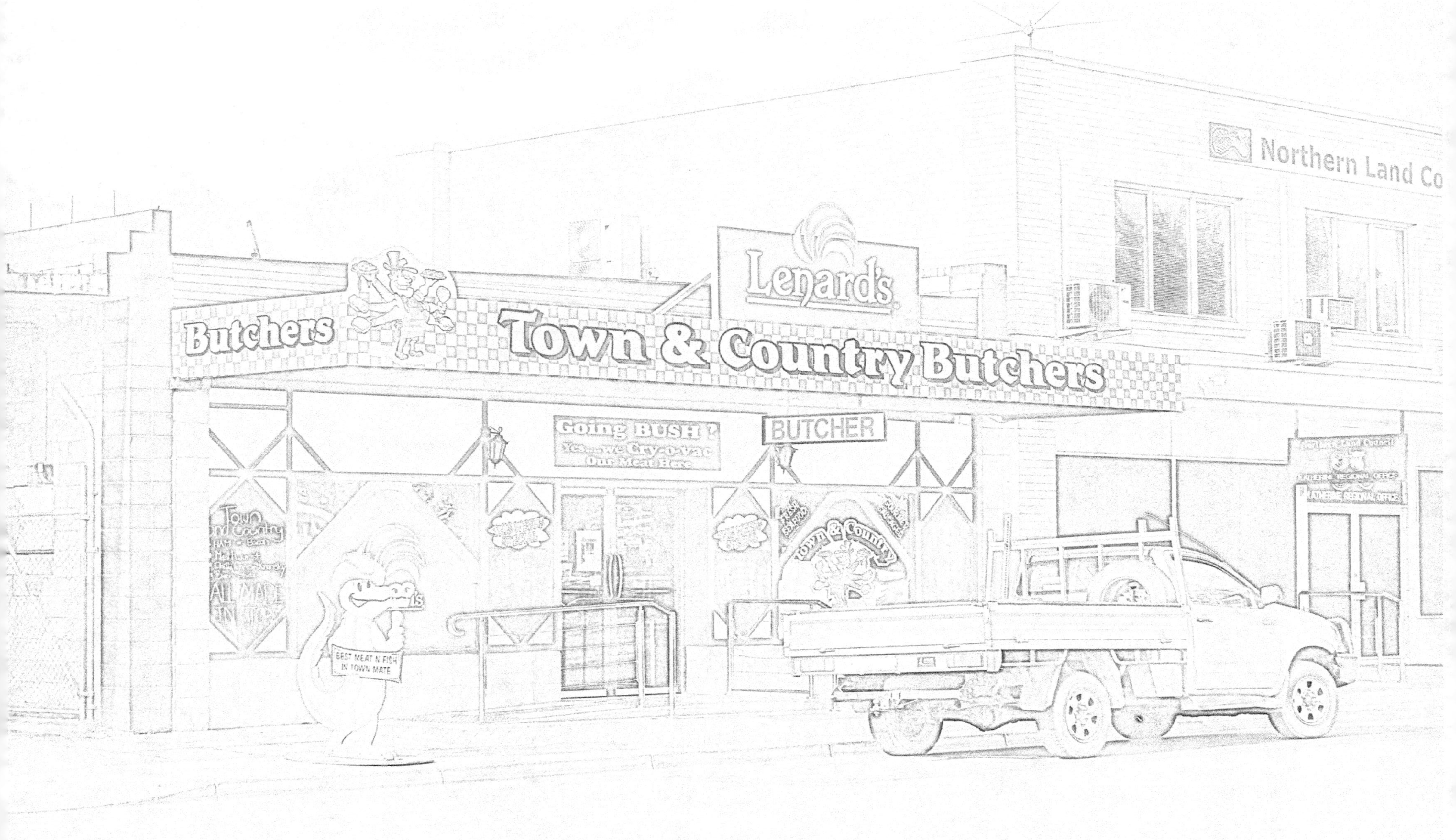
Northern Land Co
Lenard's
Butchers
Town & Country Butchers
Going BUSH ?
Ye...we Cry-o-vac
Our Meat Here
BUTCHER
ALL MADE IN STORE
Town & Country
BEST MEAT N FISH IN TOWN MATE

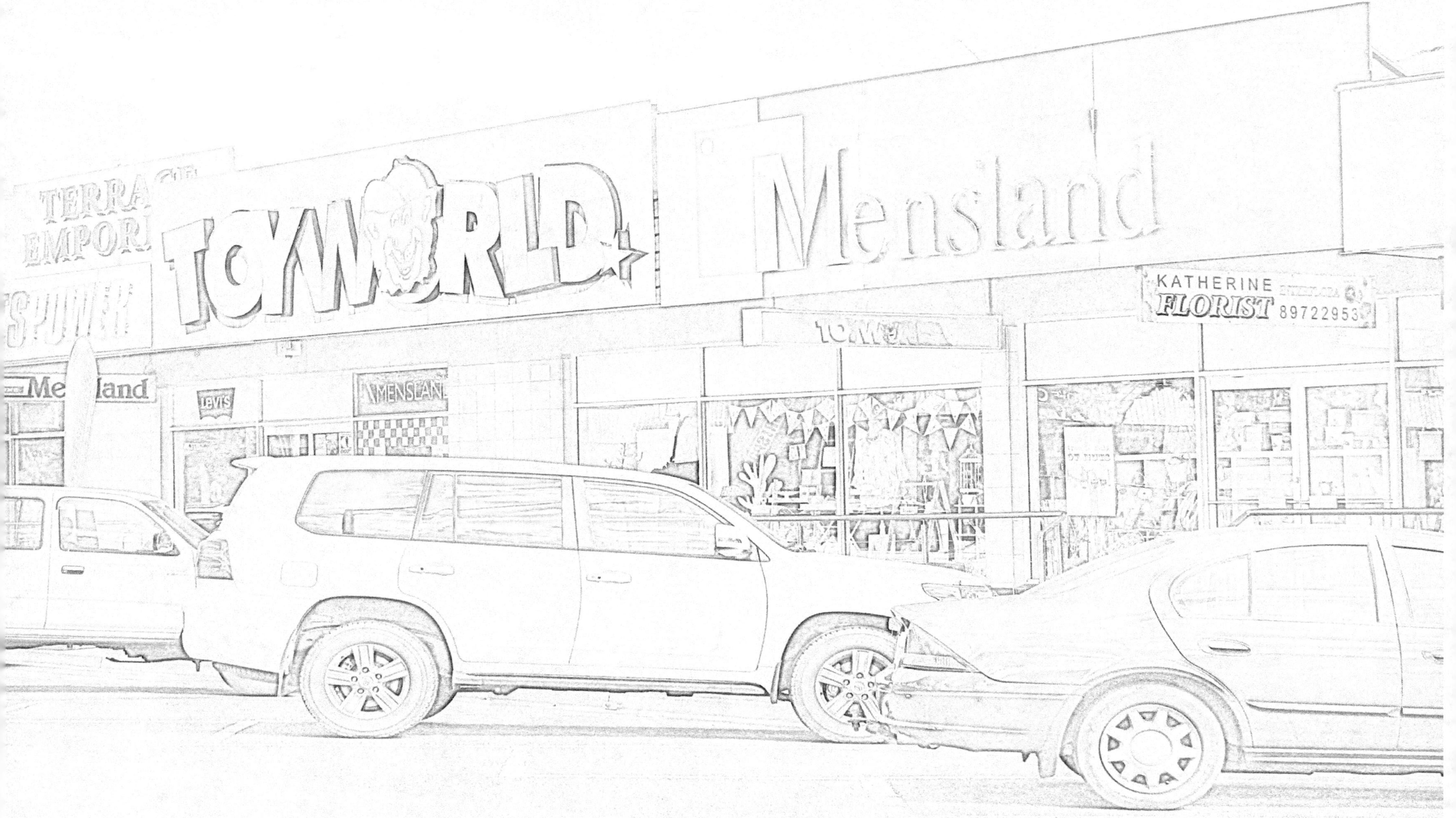
TOYWORLD
Mensland
KATHERINE
FLORIST
89722953
Levi's
MENSLAN
TOYW
Me land

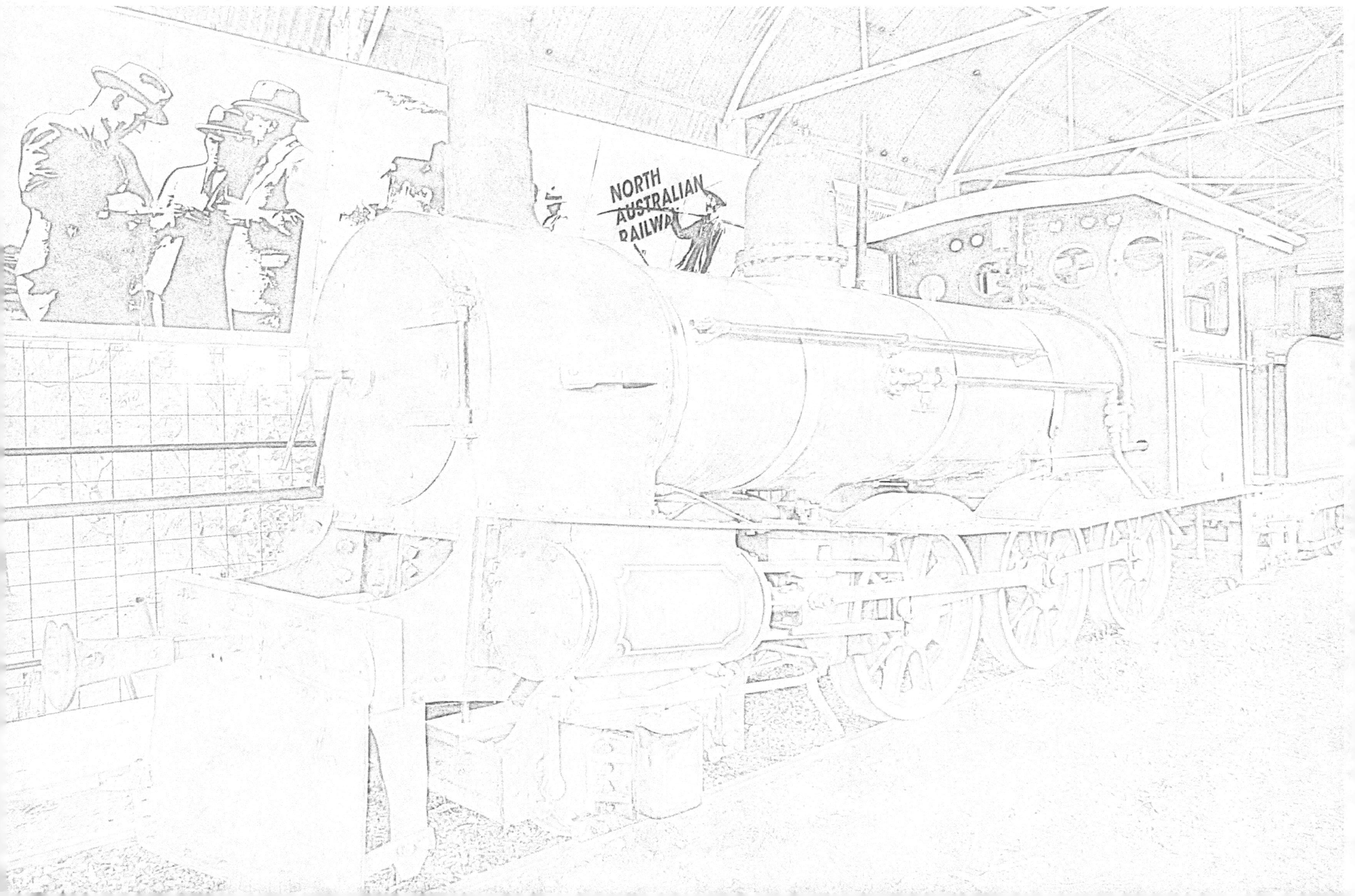
NORTH
AUSTRALIAN

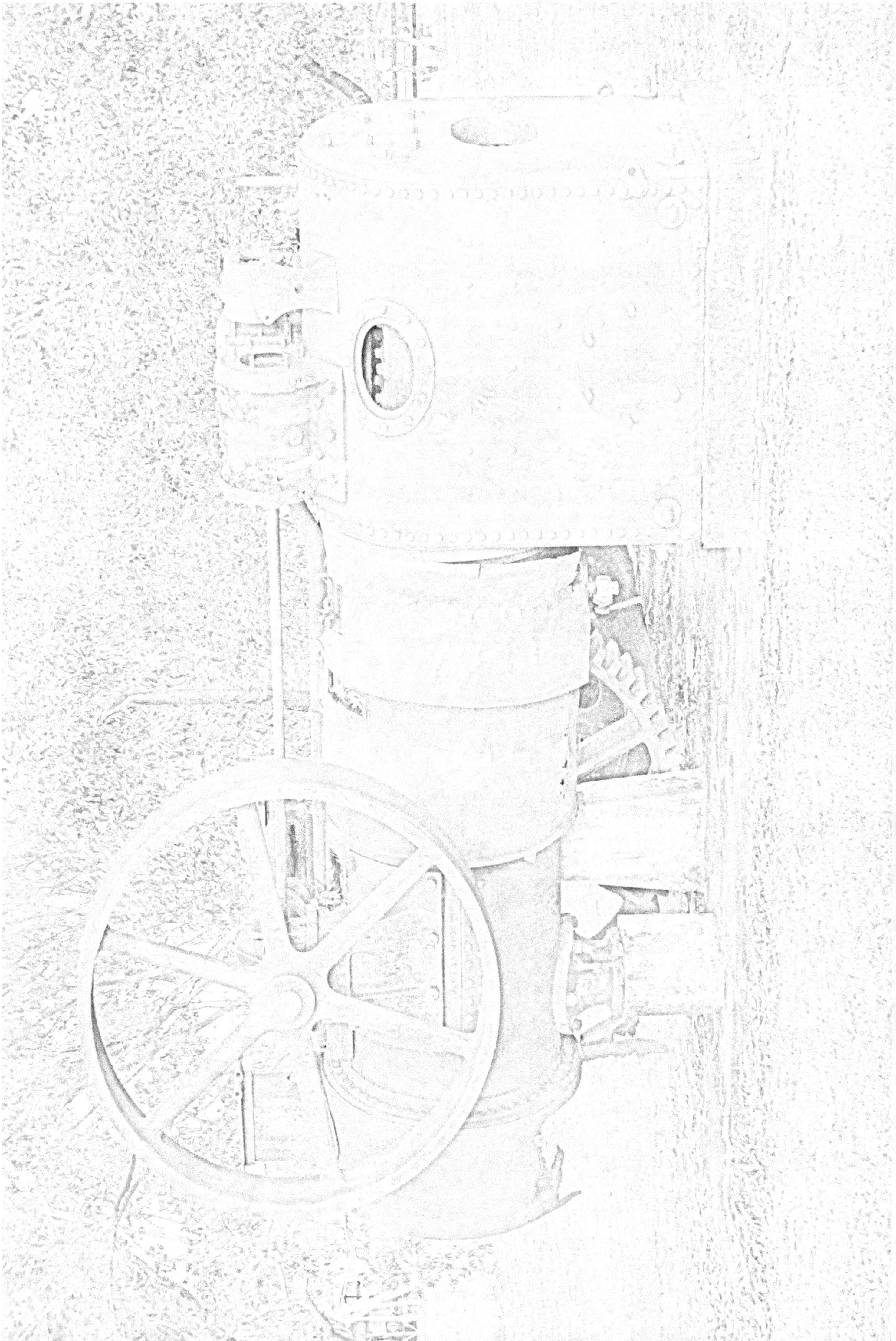

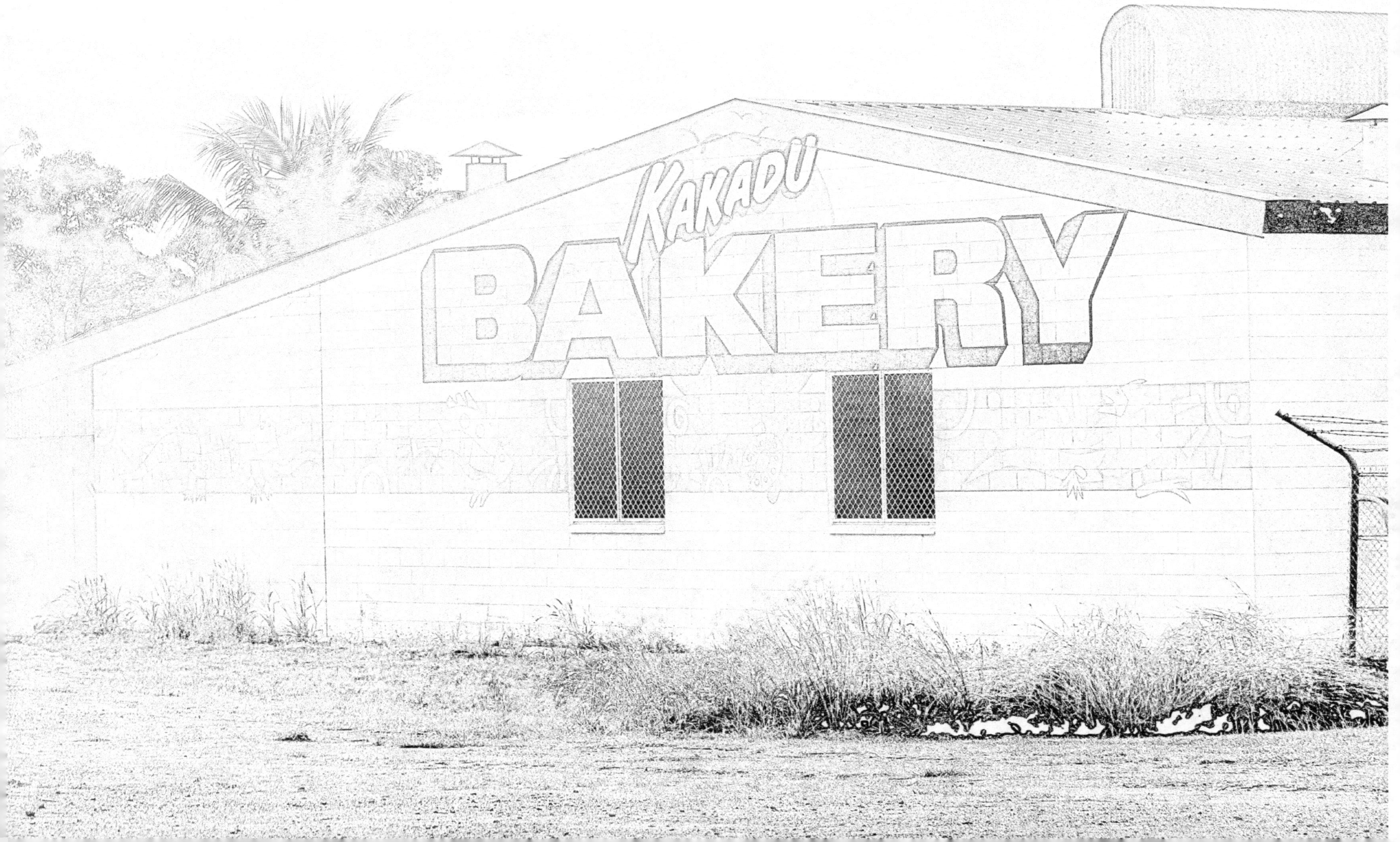
KAKADU
BAKERY

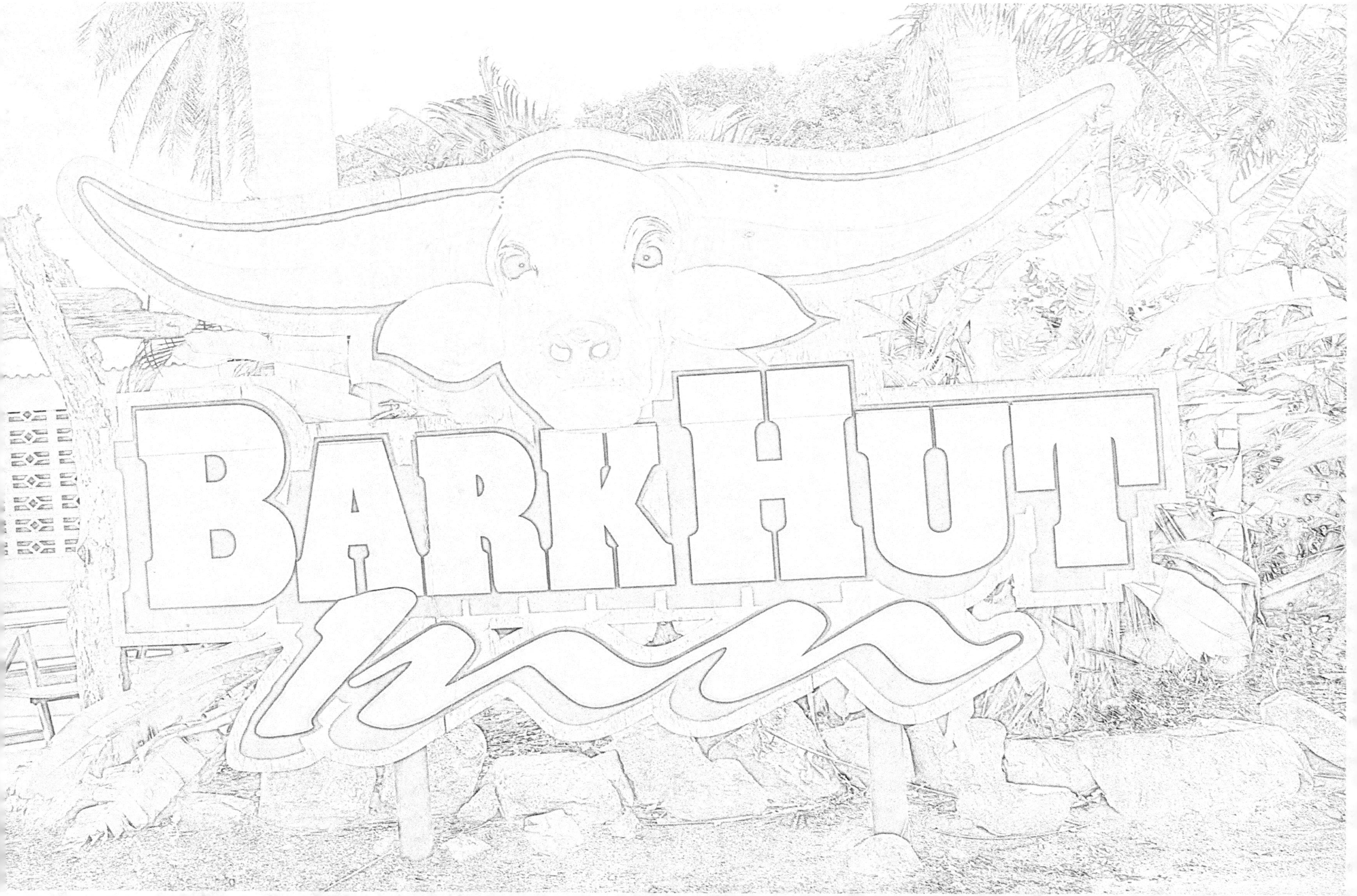
BARKHUT

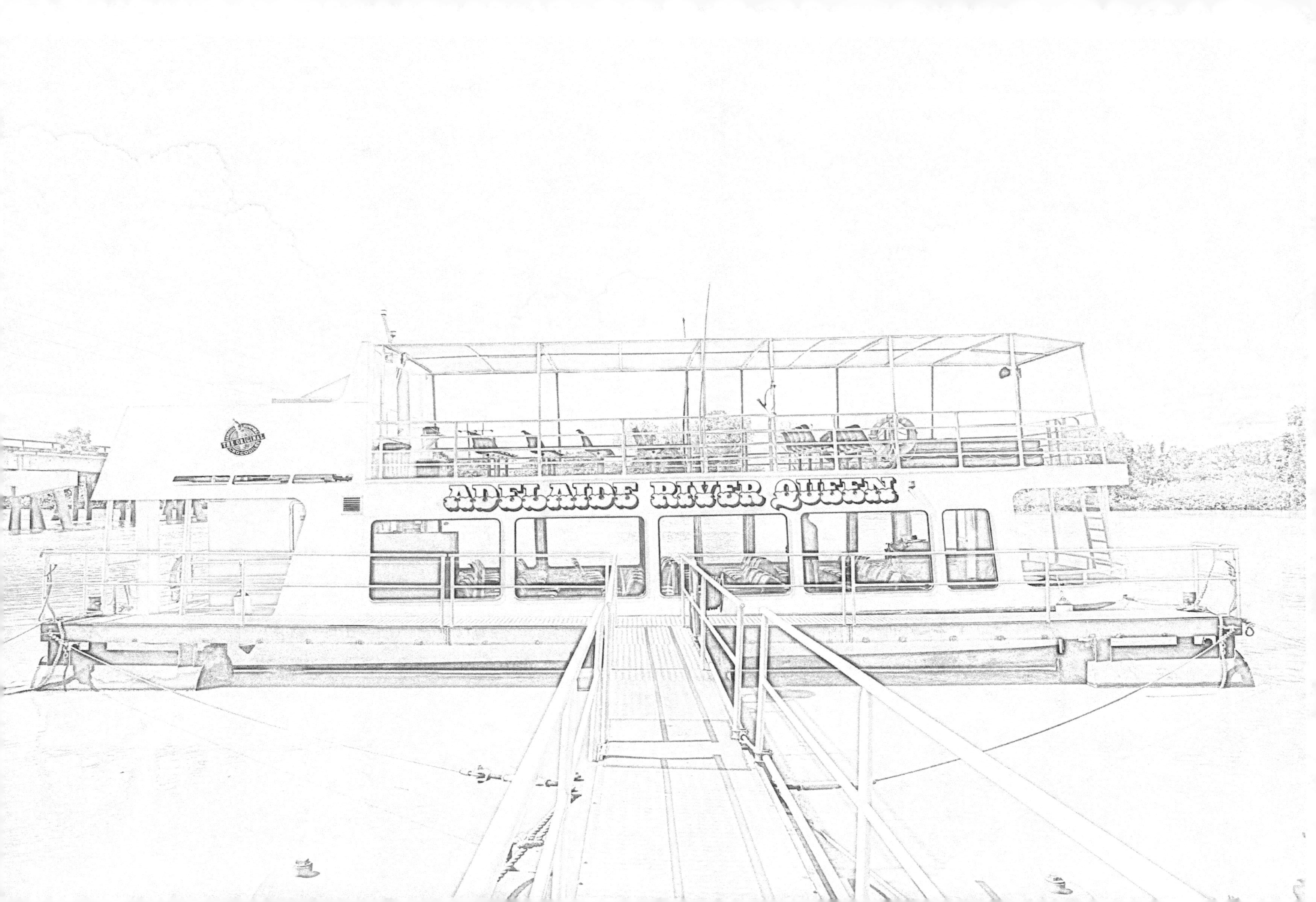
ADELAIDE RIVER QUEEN
THE ORIGINAL

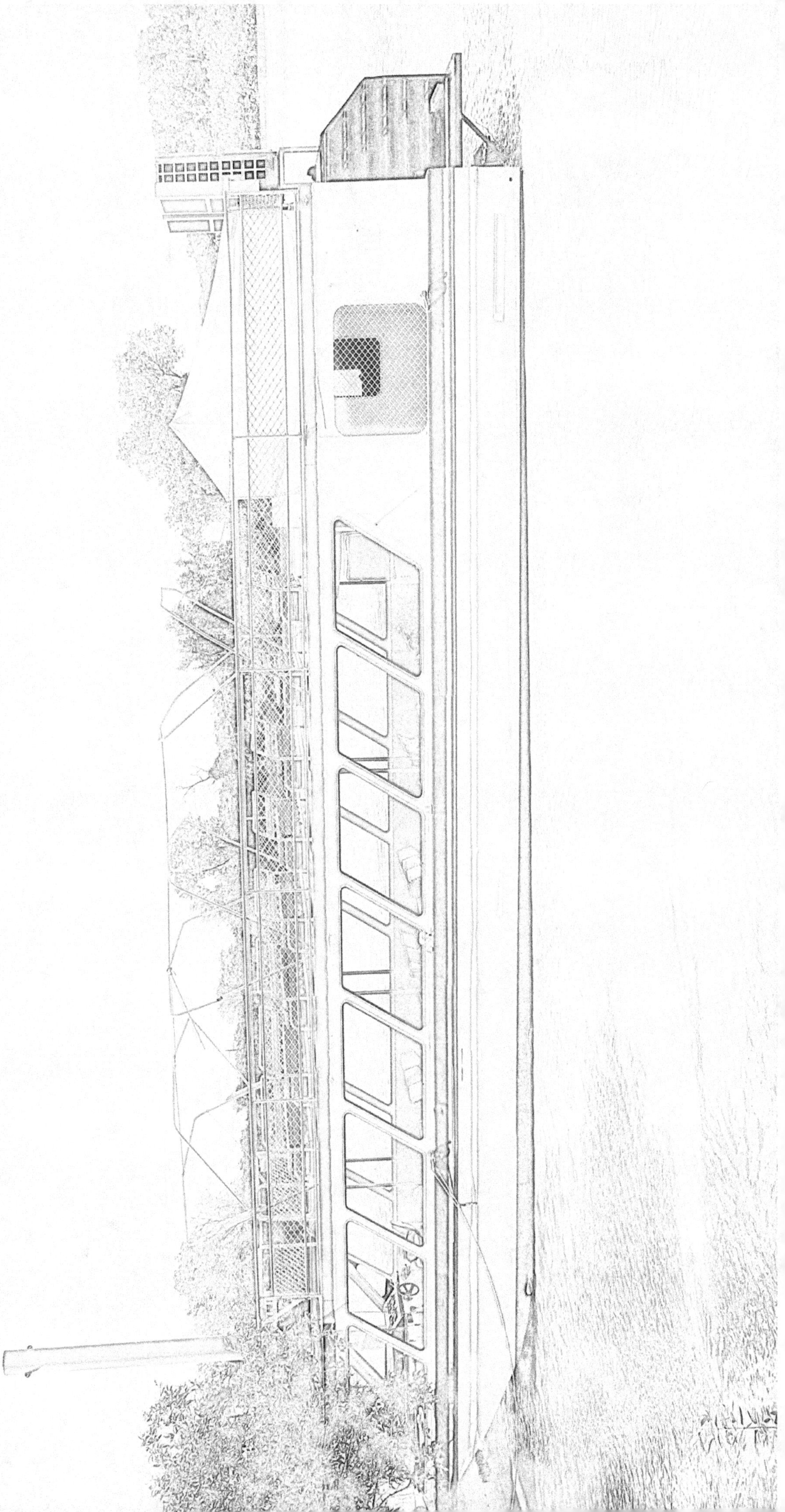

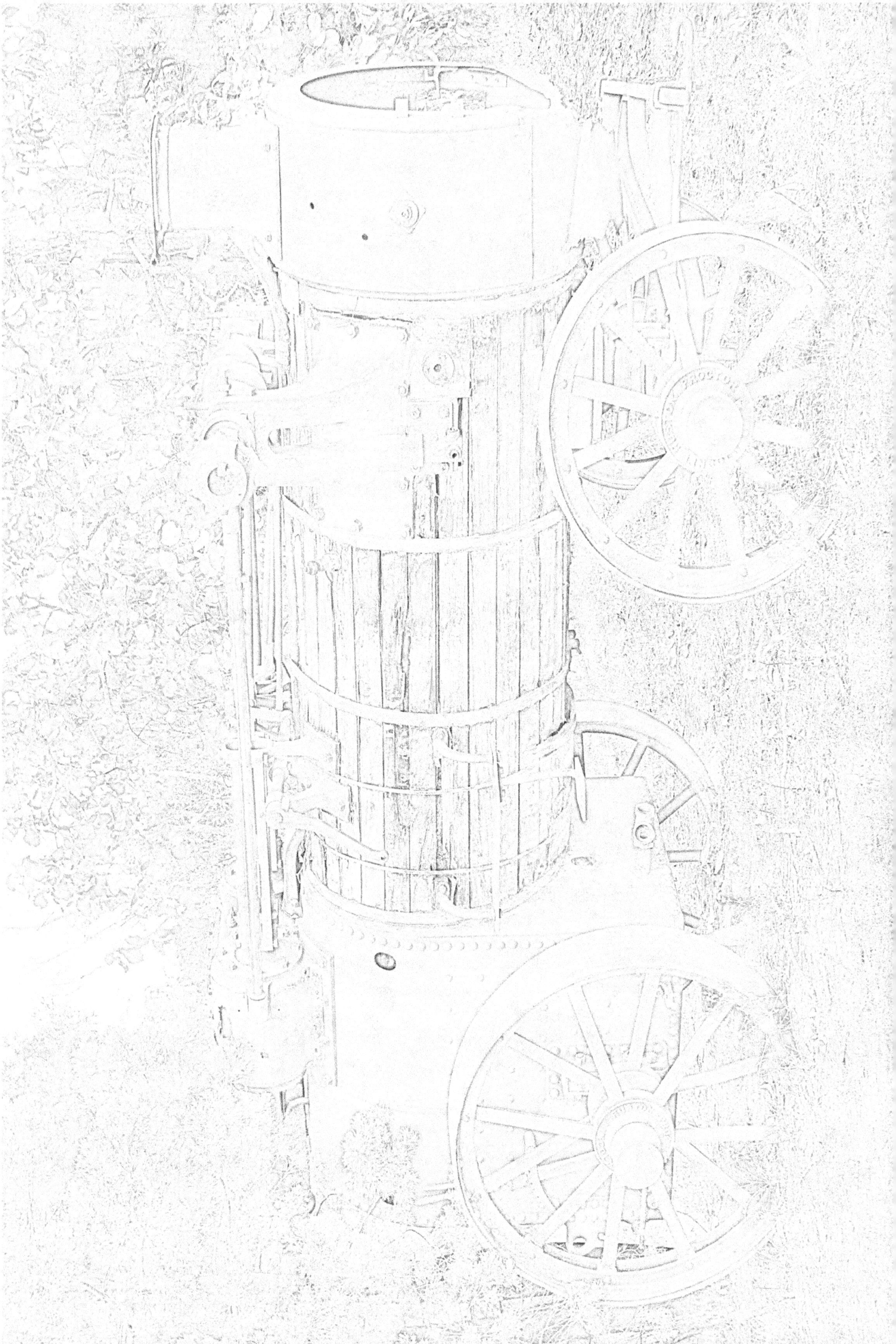

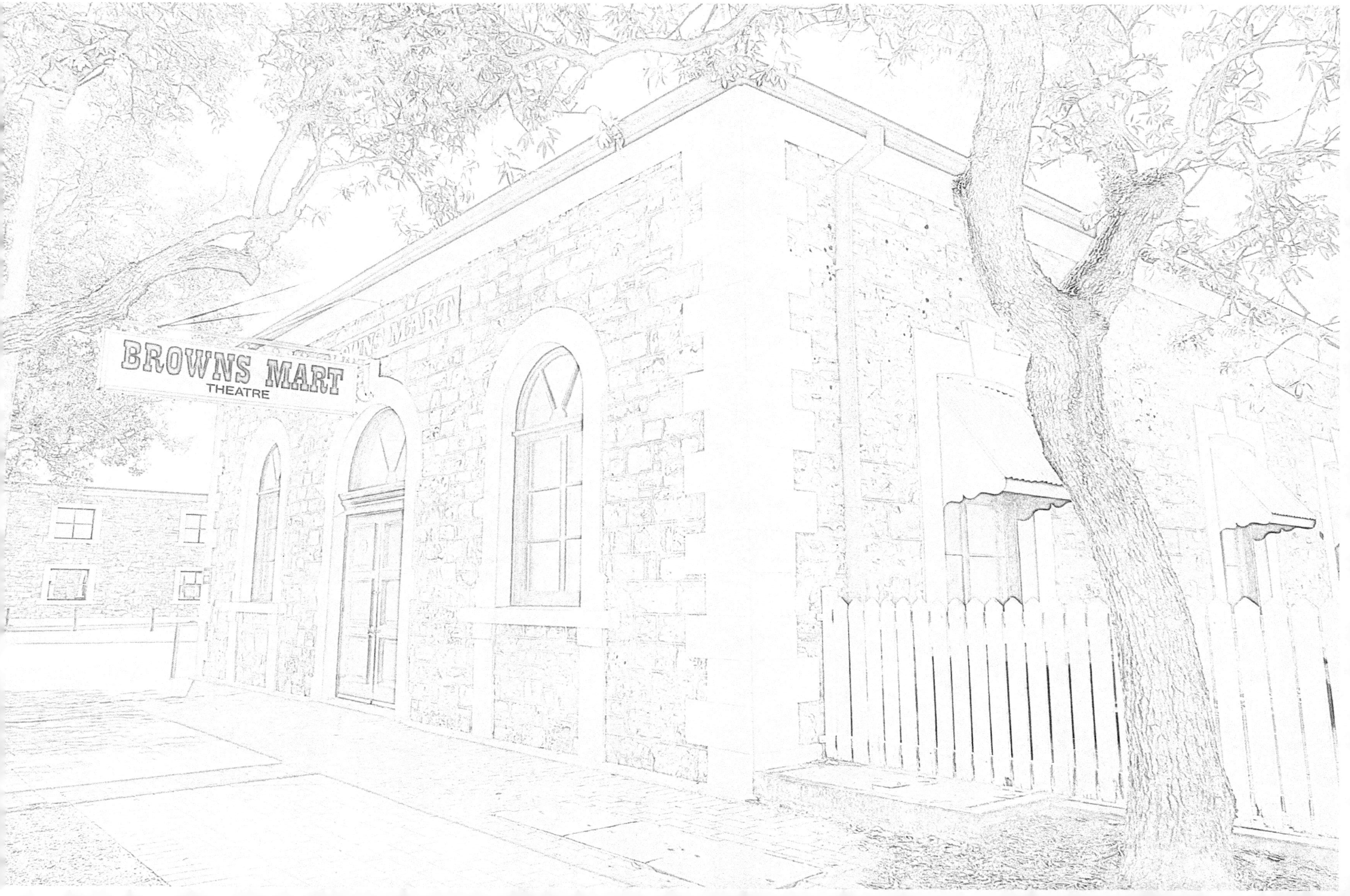
BROWNS MART
THEATRE

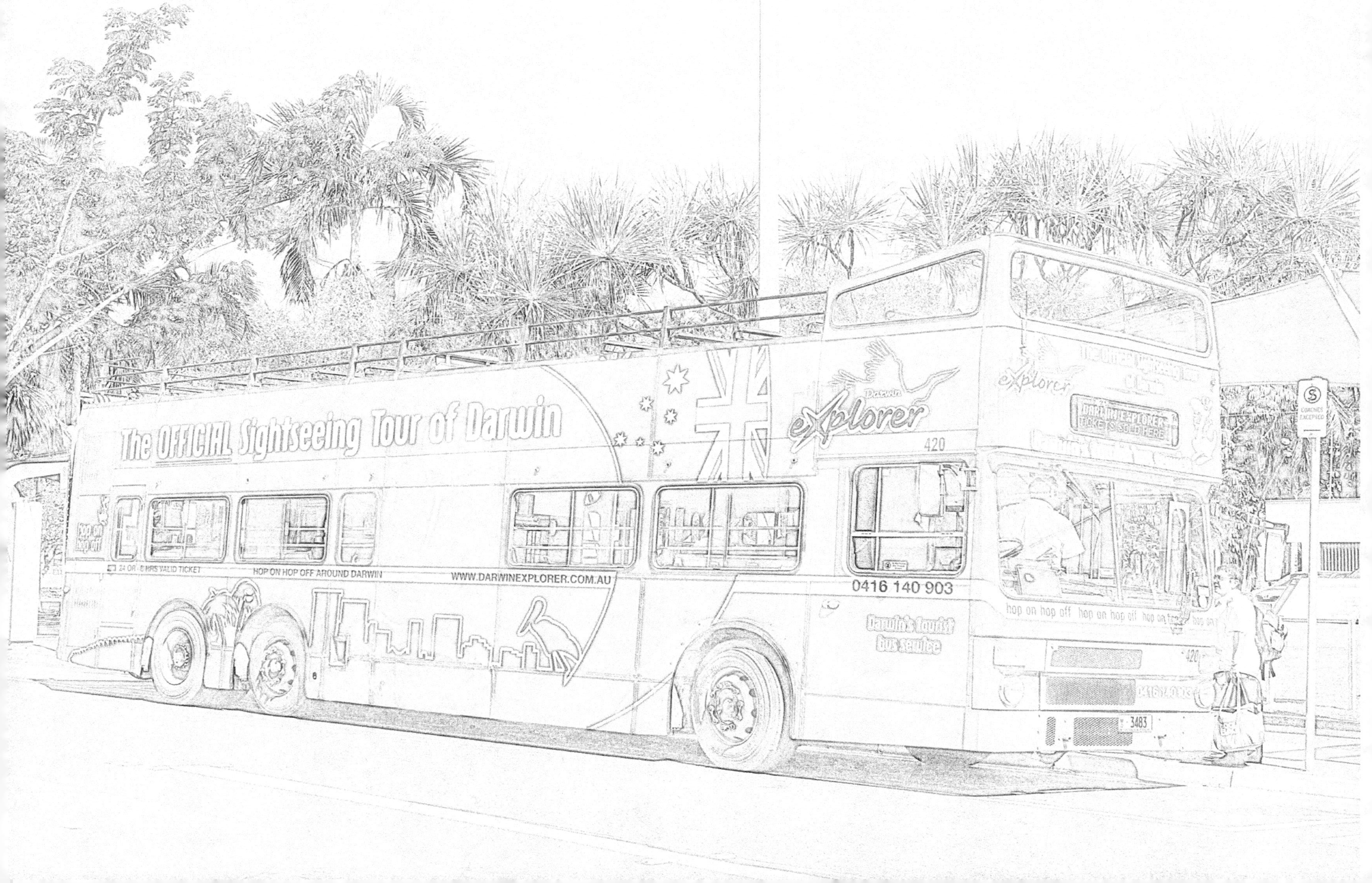
The OFFICIAL Sightseeing Tour of Darwin
Darwin eXplorer
420
DARWIN EXPLORER TICKETS SOLD HERE
24 OR 8 HRS VALID TICKET
HOP ON HOP OFF AROUND DARWIN
WWW.DARWINEXPLORER.COM.AU
0416 140 903
Darwin's tourist bus service
hop on hop off hop on hop off
COACHES EXCEPTED
3483

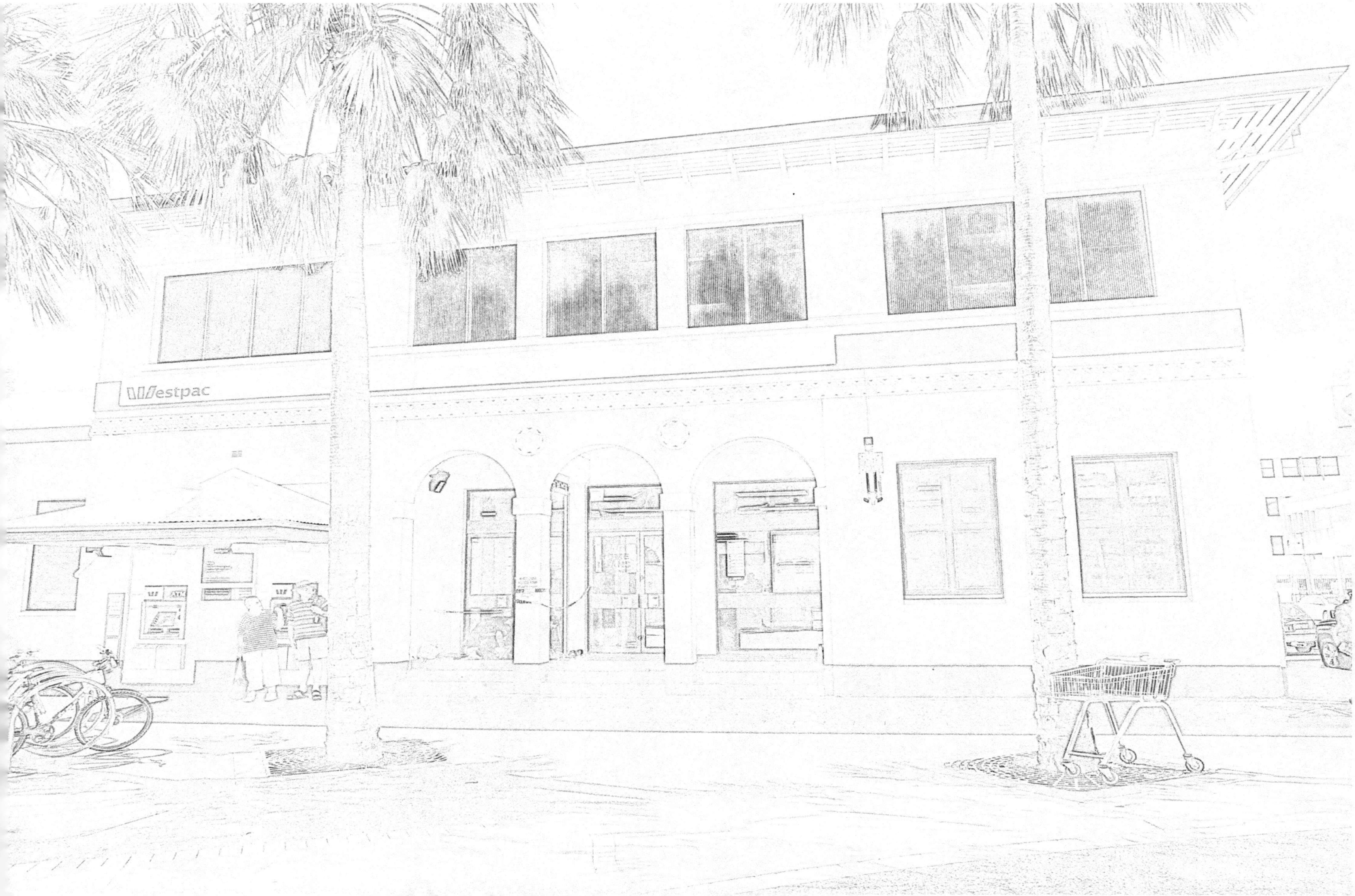
Westpac

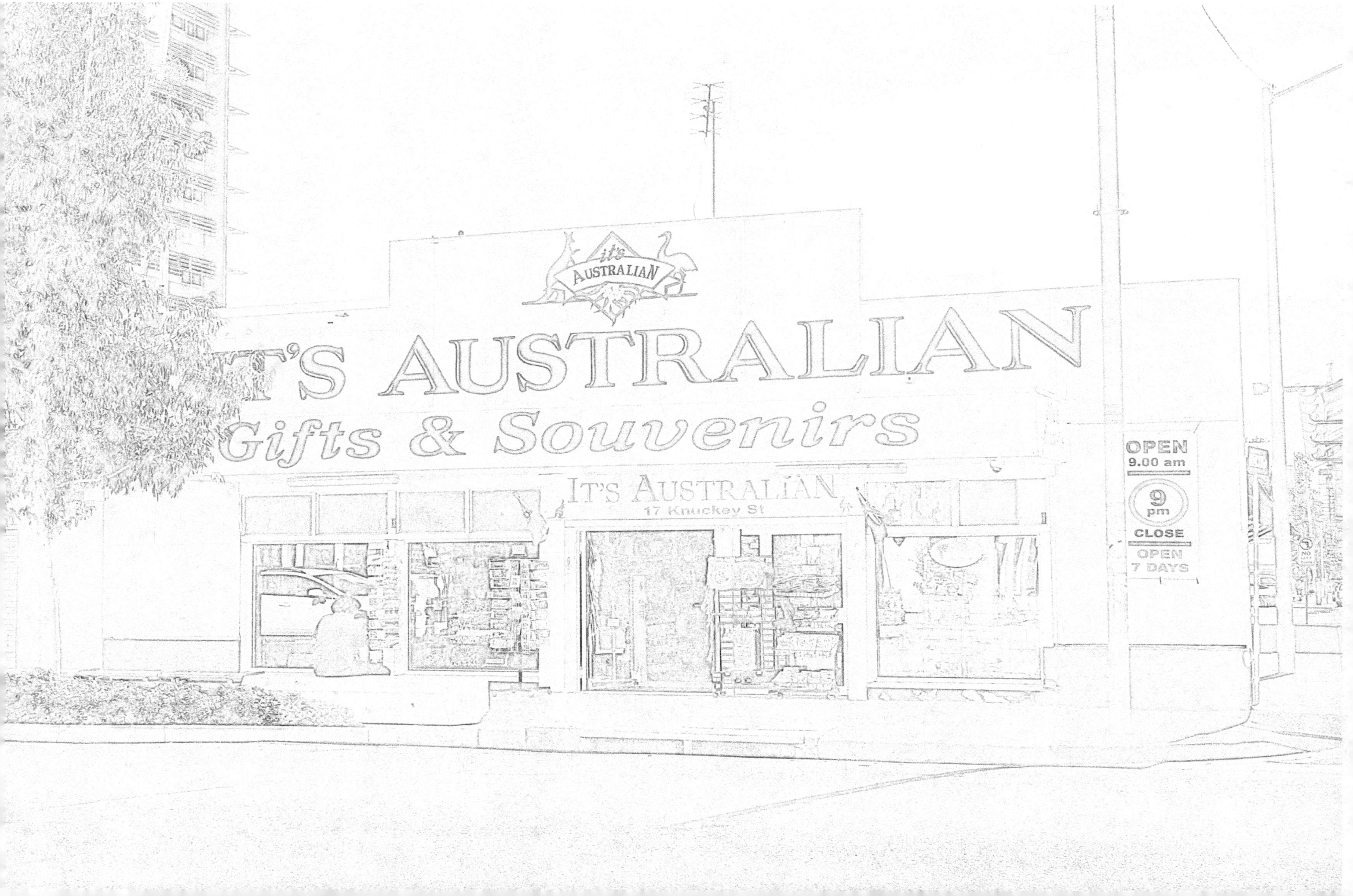
it's AUSTRALIAN
IT'S AUSTRALIAN
Gifts & Souvenirs
IT'S AUSTRALIAN
17 Knuckey St
OPEN
9.00 am
9
pm
CLOSE
OPEN
7 DAYS

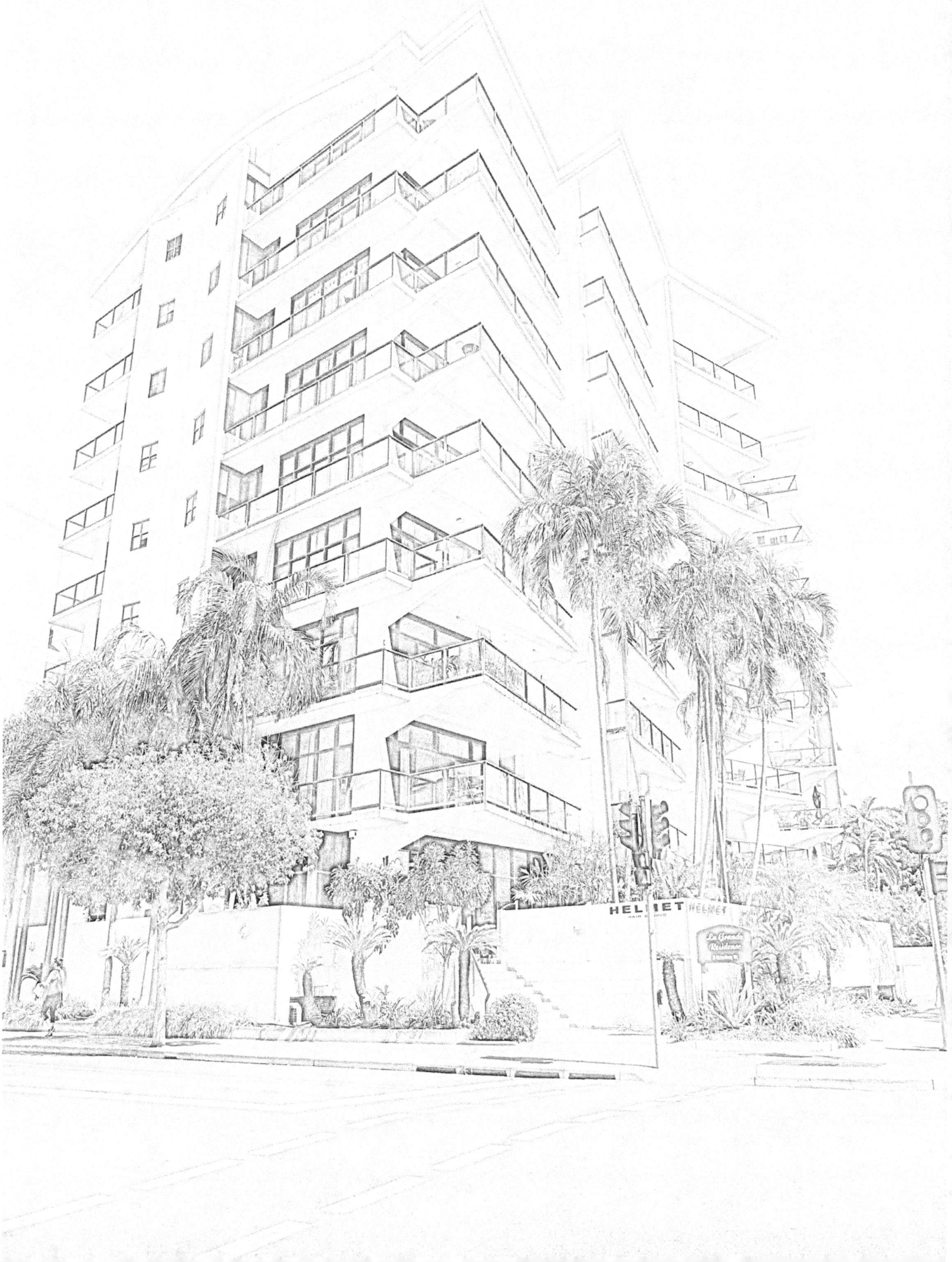
HELMET

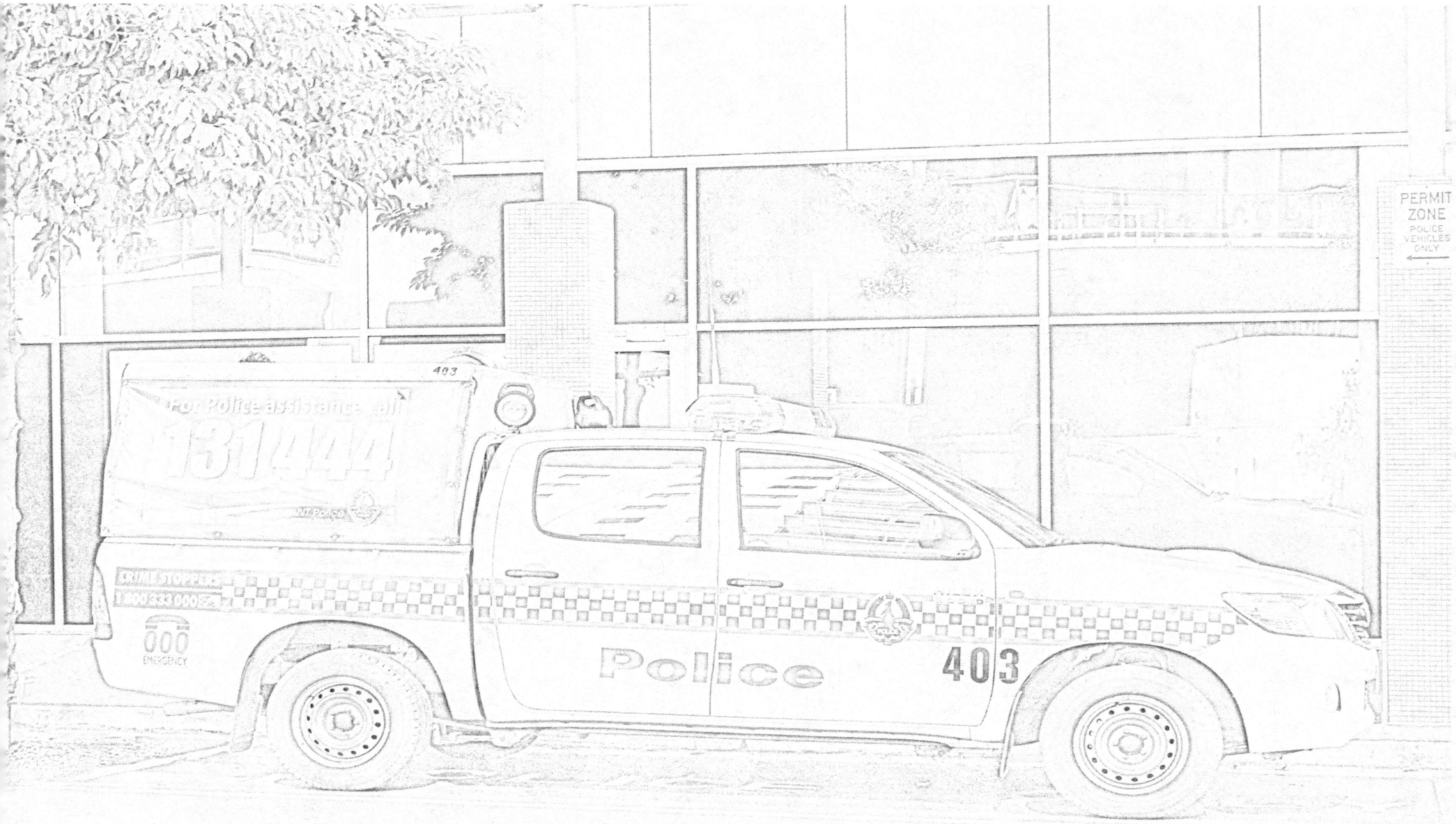
PERMIT ZONE
POLICE VEHICLES ONLY
For Police assistance call
131444
NT Police
403
CRIME STOPPERS
1800 333 000
000
EMERGENCY
Police
403

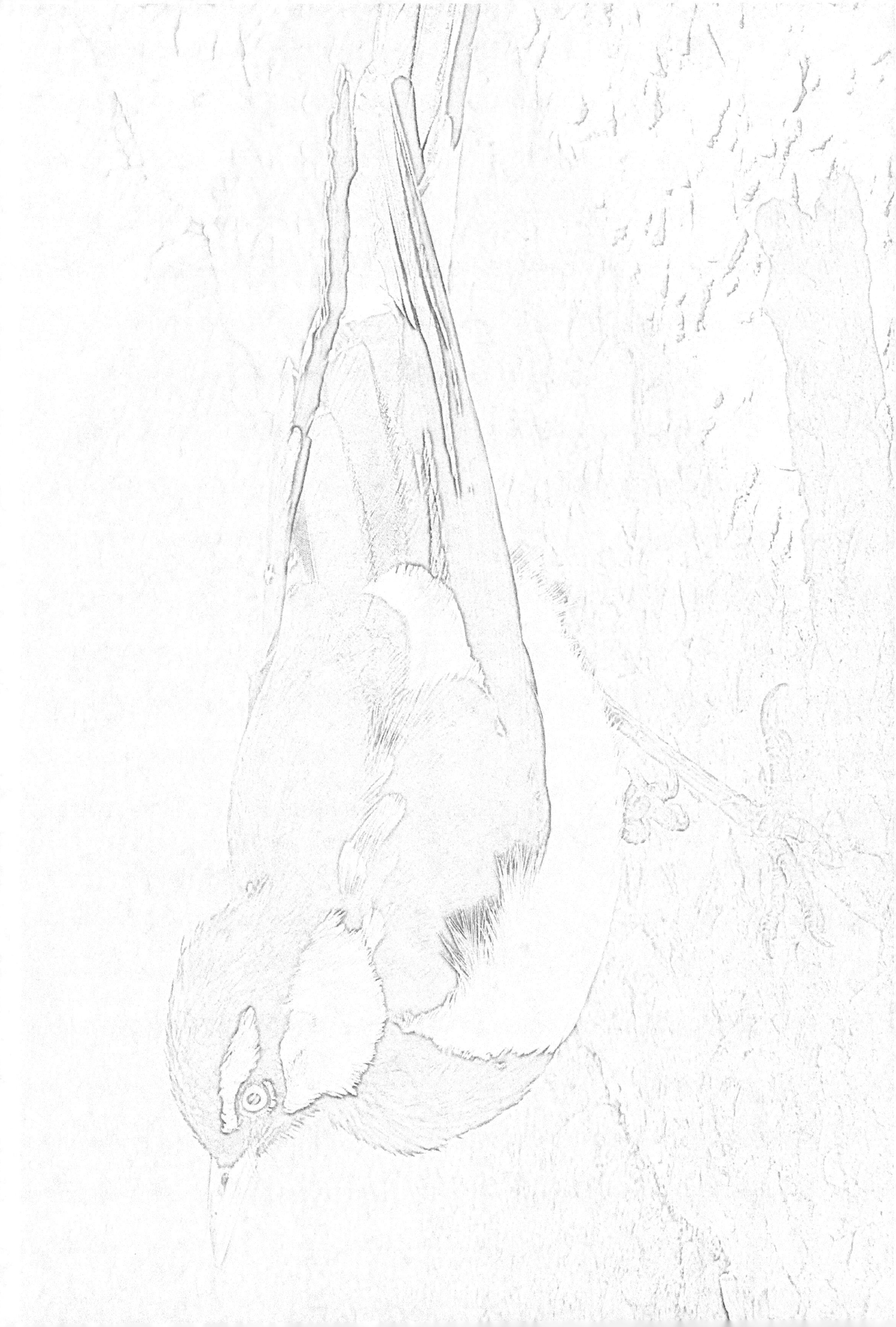

ST. MARY'S
CATHEDRAL

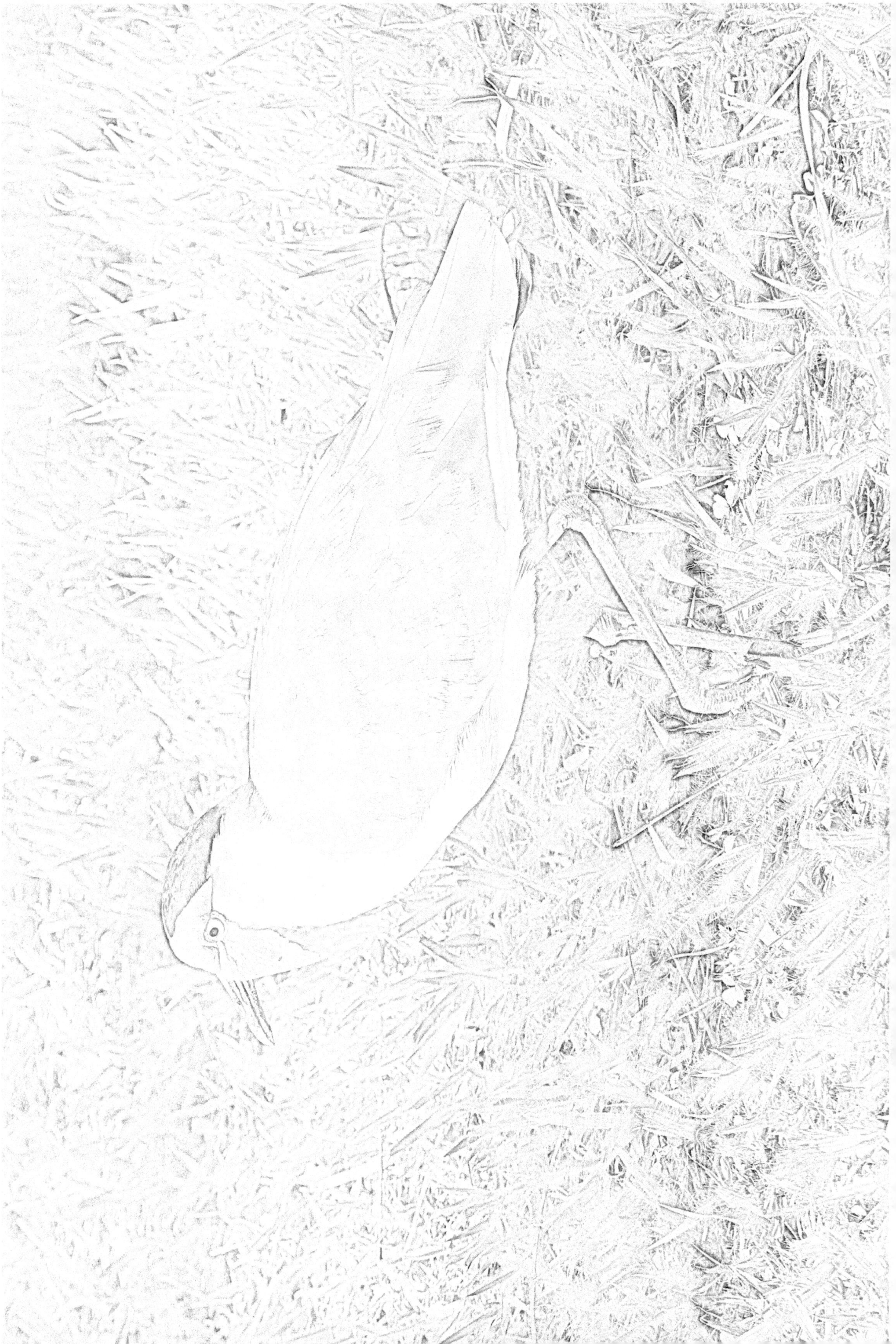

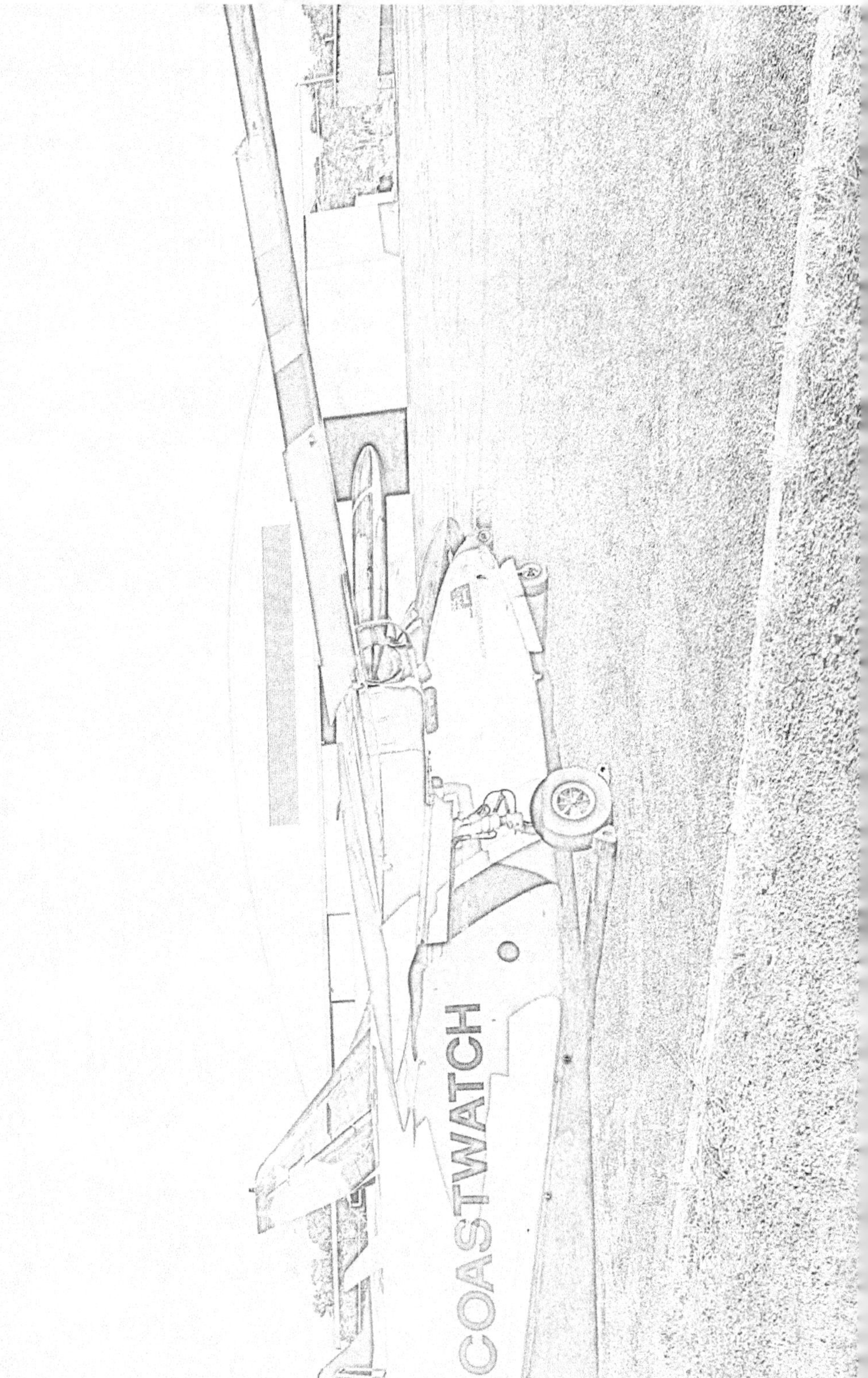
COASTWATCH

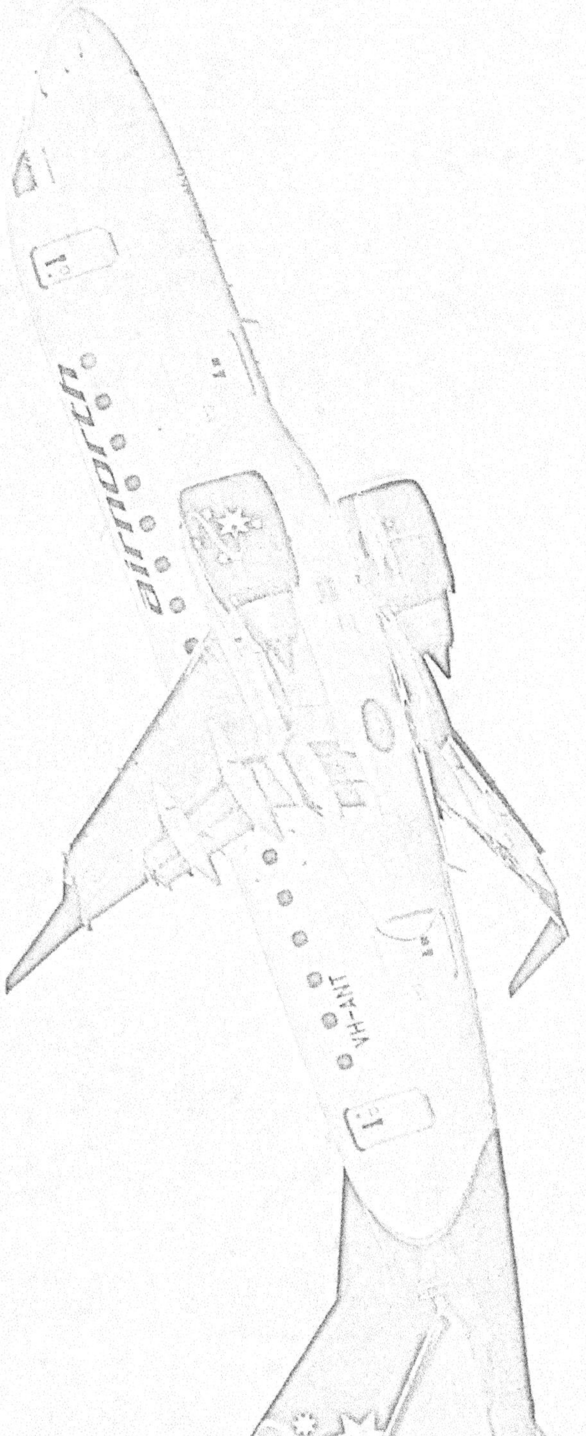
airnorth
VH-ANT

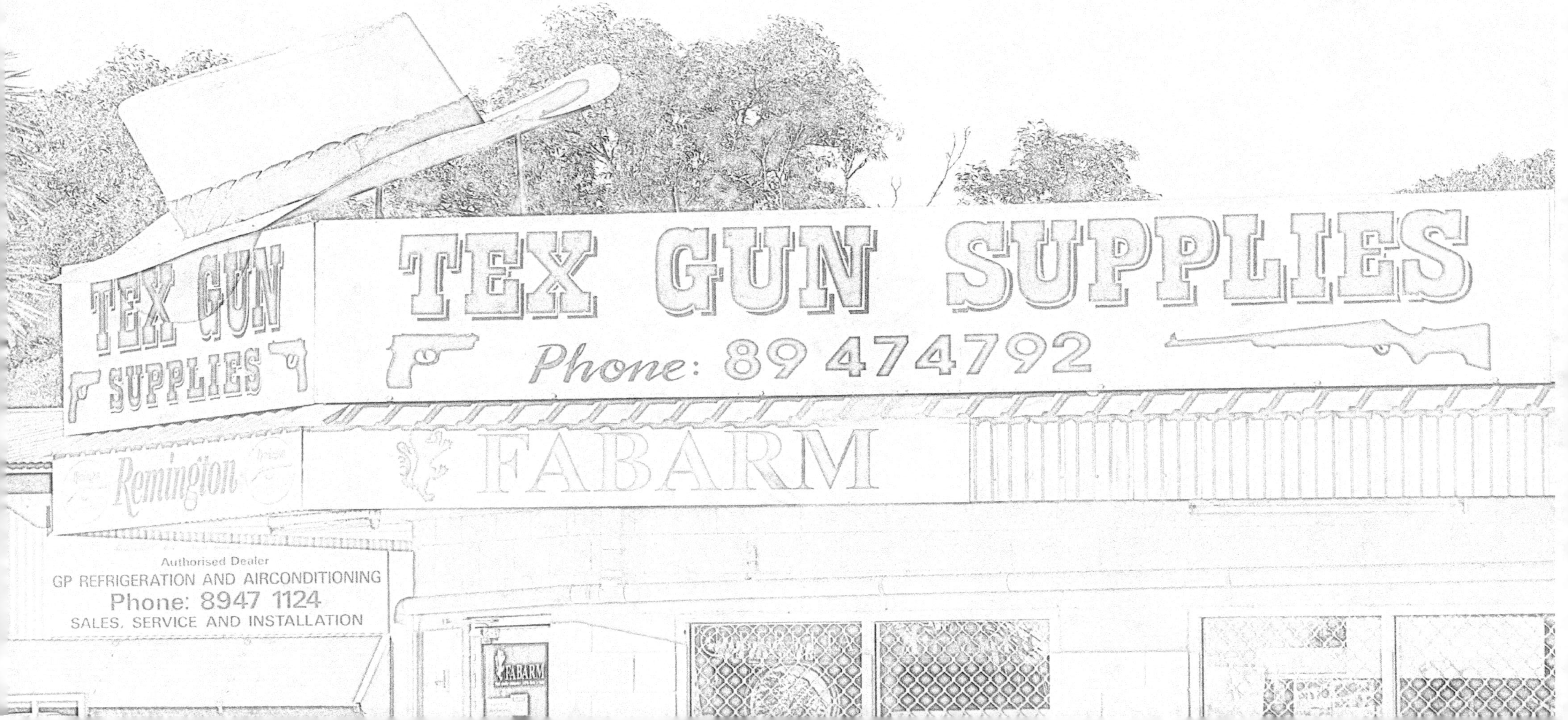
TEX GUN
SUPPLIES
TEX GUN SUPPLIES
Phone: 89 474792
Remington
FABARM
Authorised Dealer
GP REFRIGERATION AND AIRCONDITIONING
Phone: 8947 1124
SALES, SERVICE AND INSTALLATION
FABARM

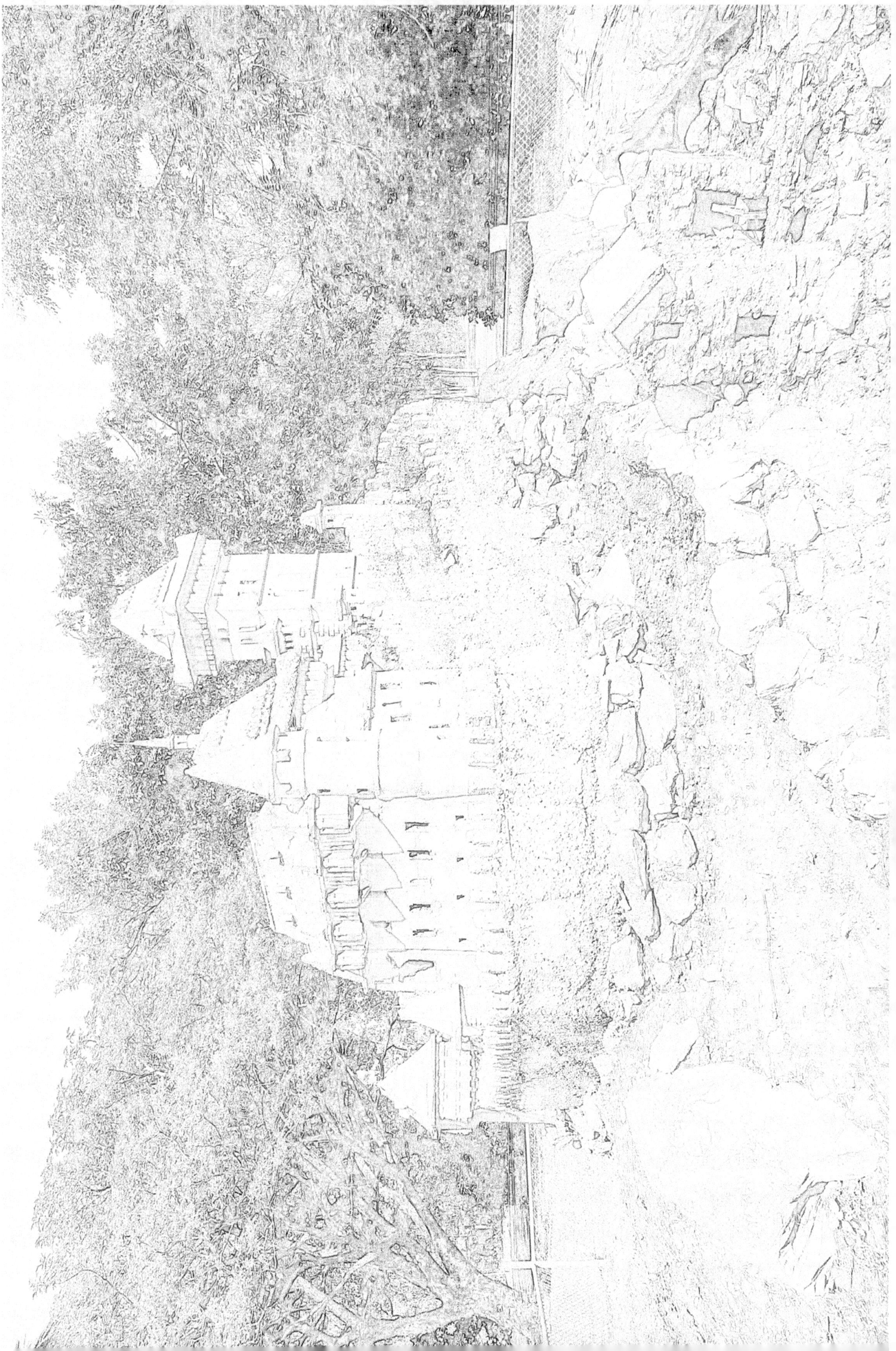

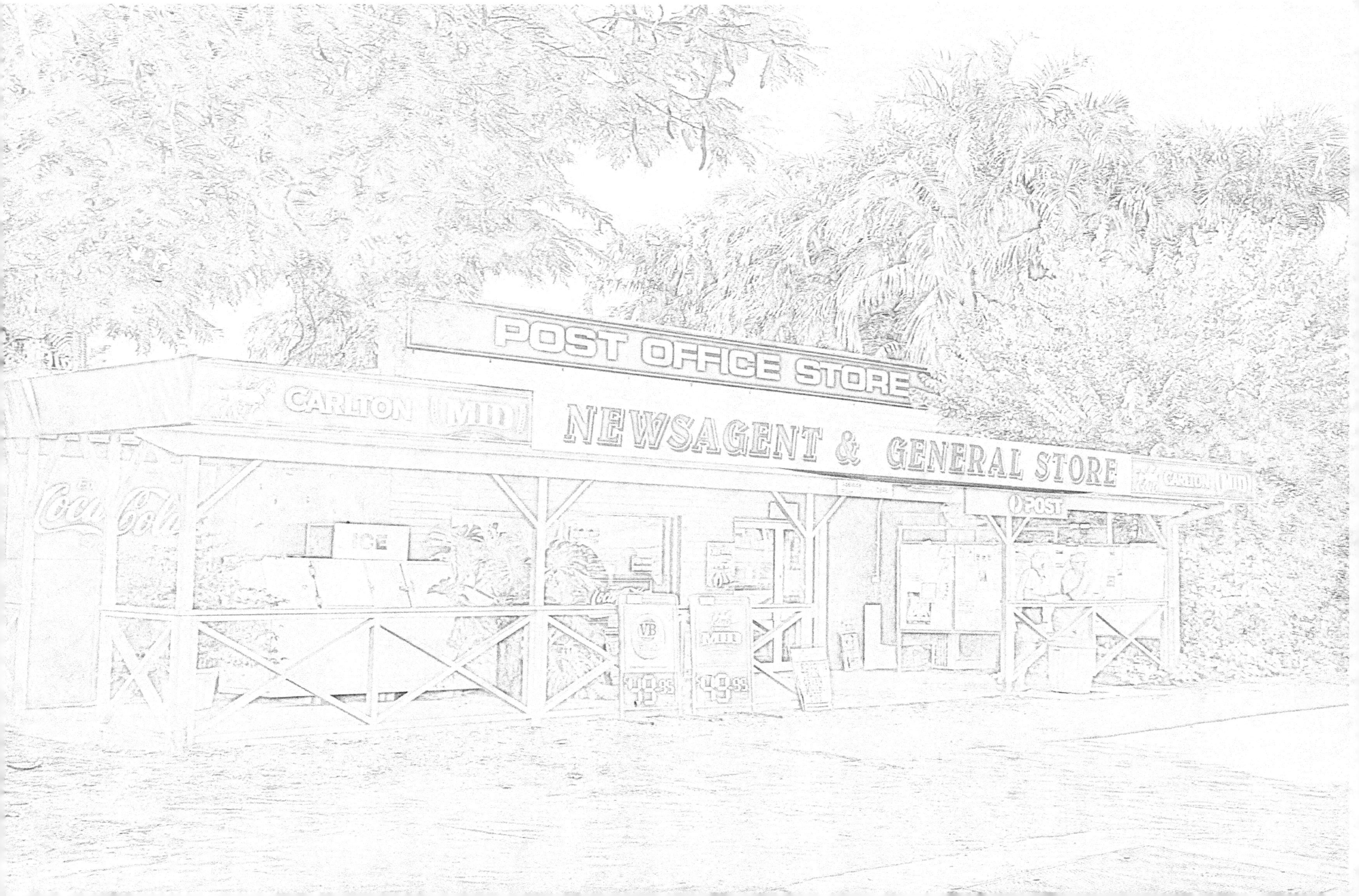
POST OFFICE STORE
NEWSAGENT & GENERAL STORE
CARLTON MID
POST
ICE
Coca-Cola
VB
MID

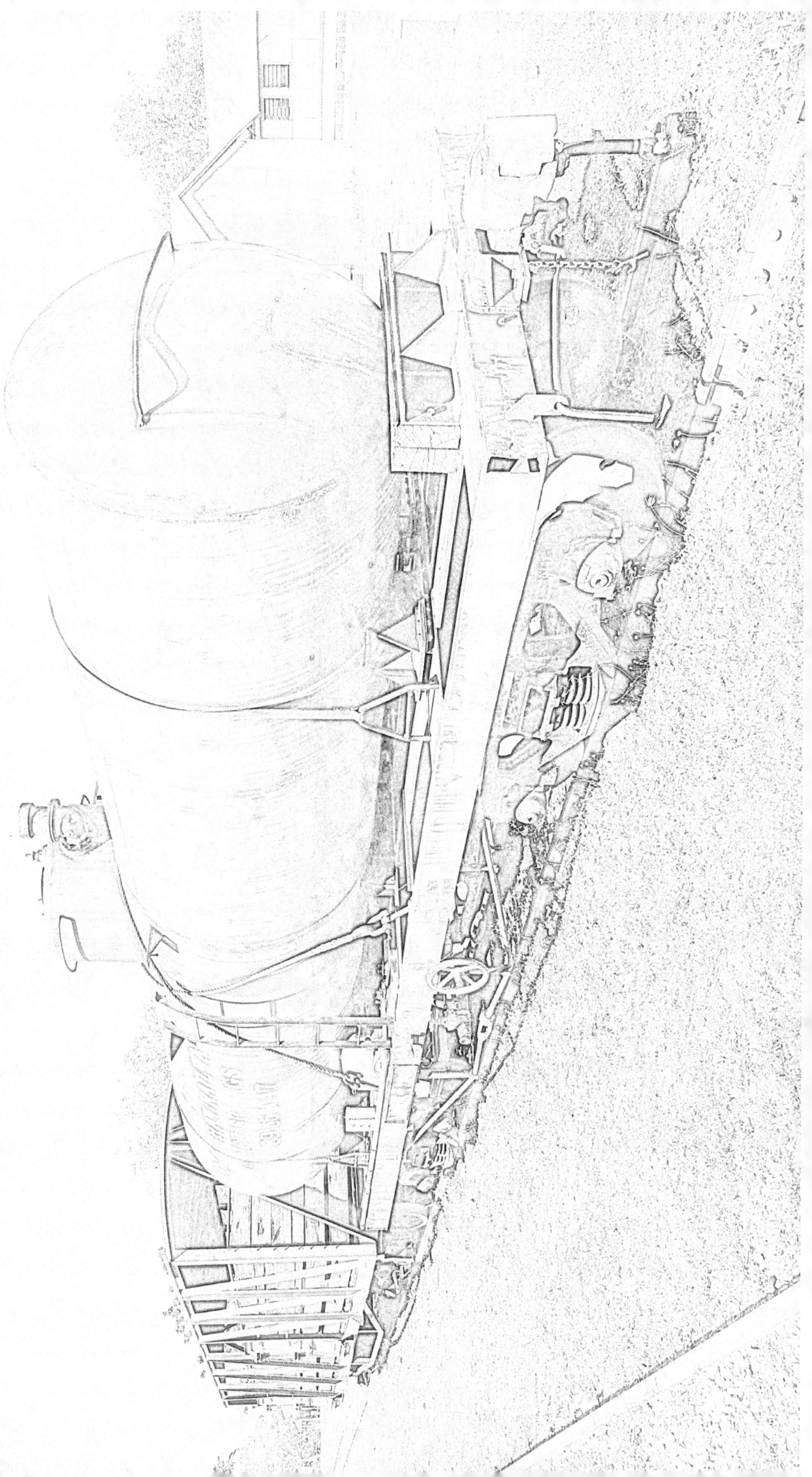

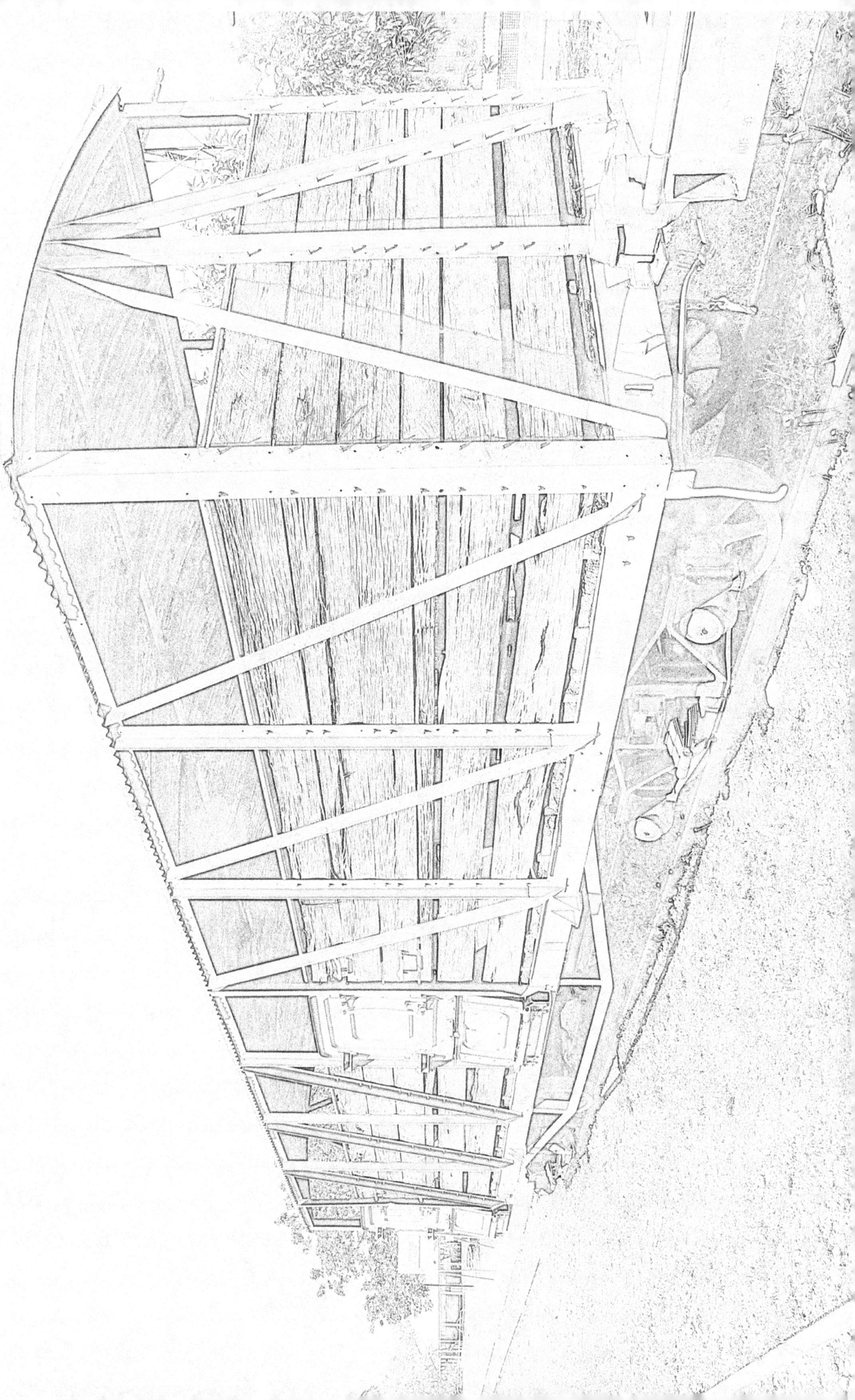

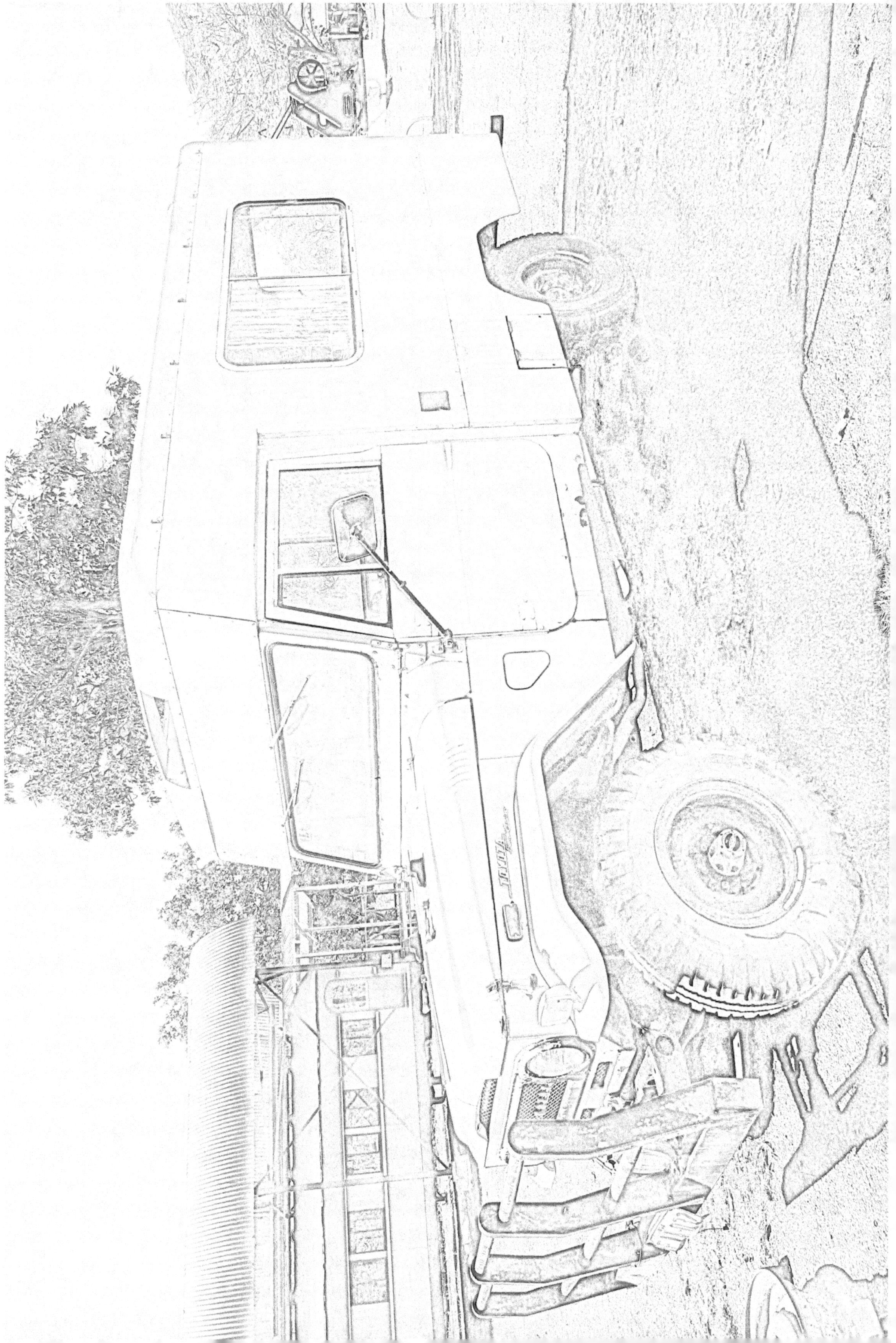

NSU·63

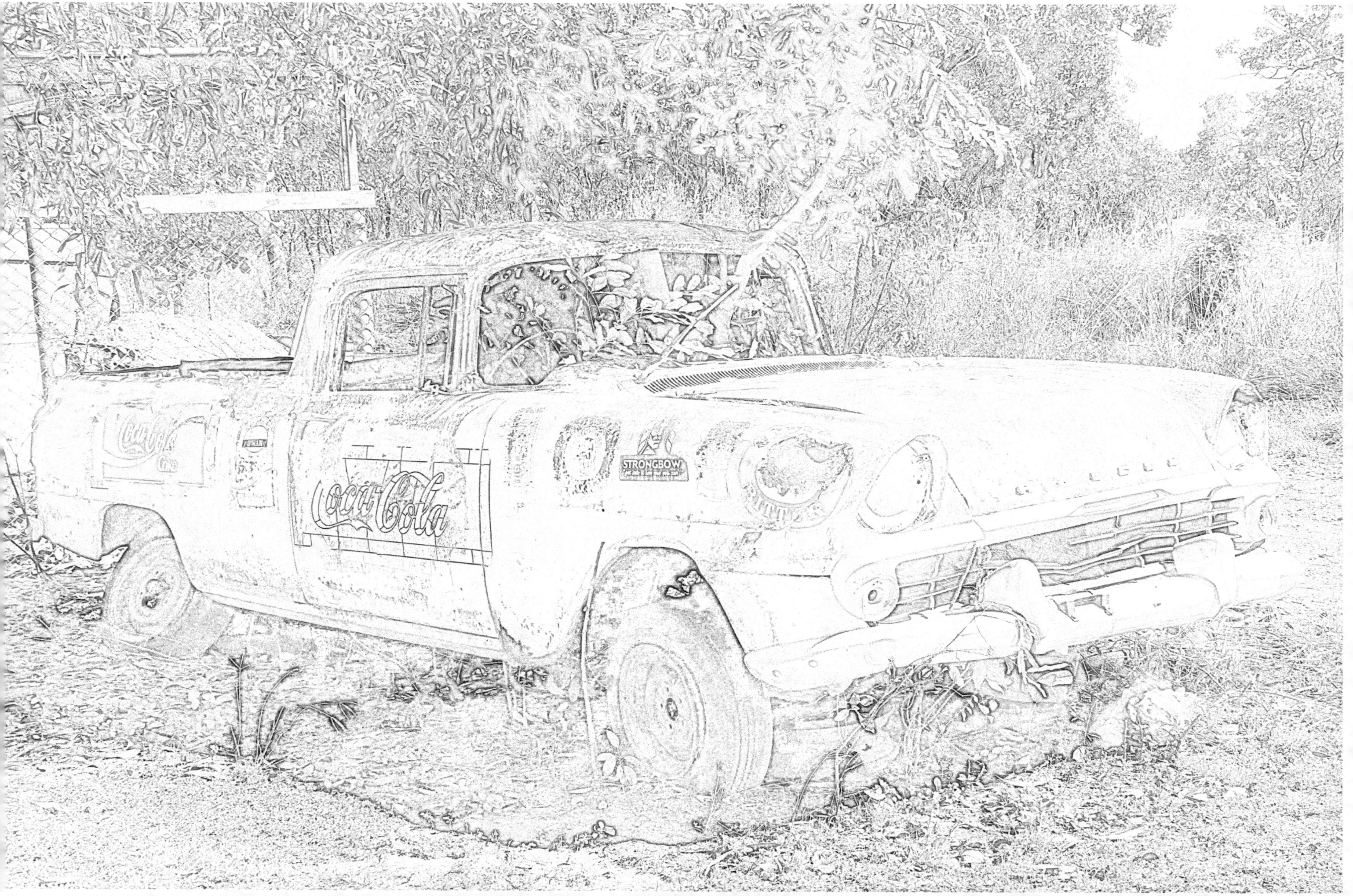
Coca-Cola
STRONGBOW

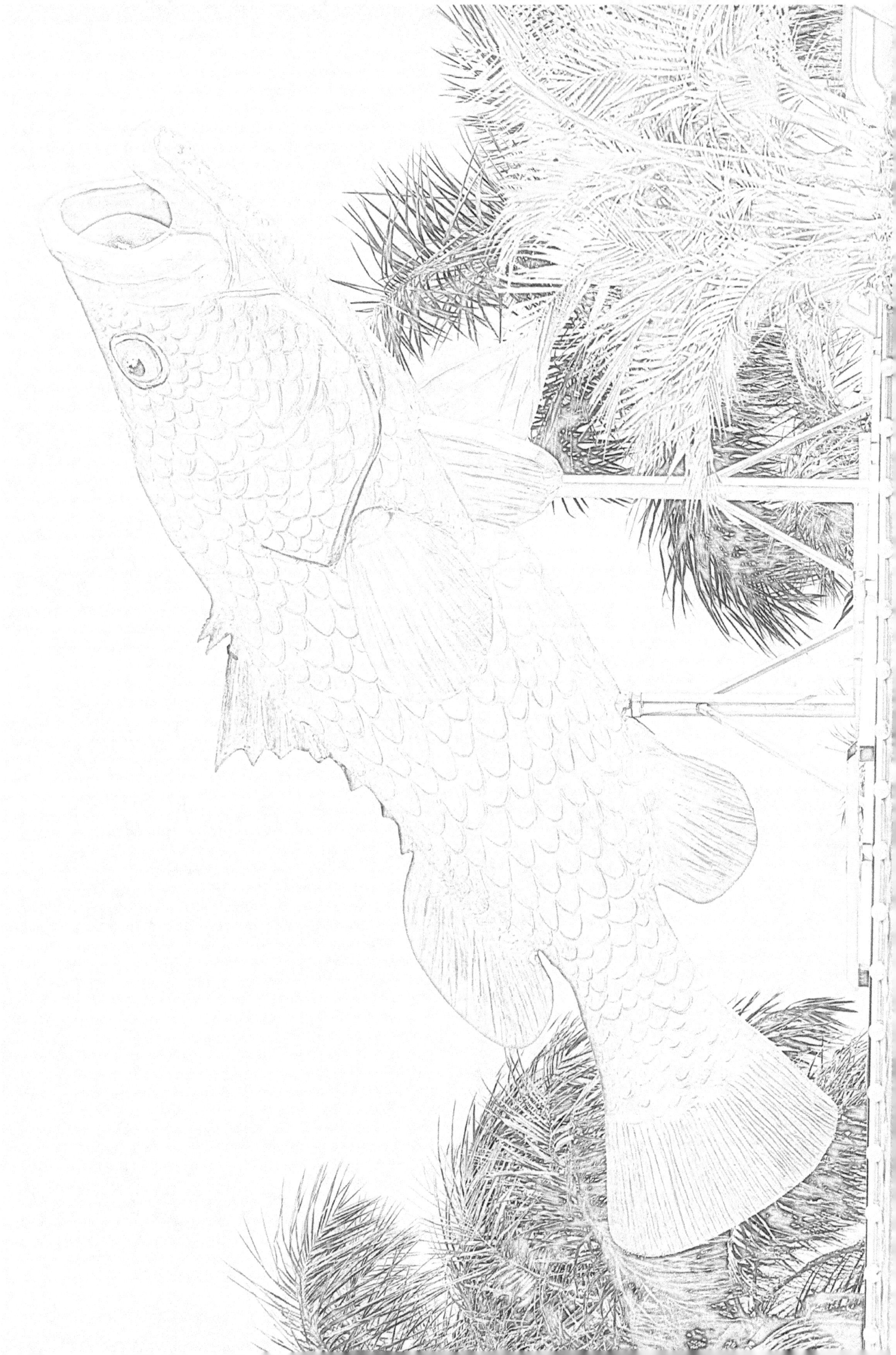

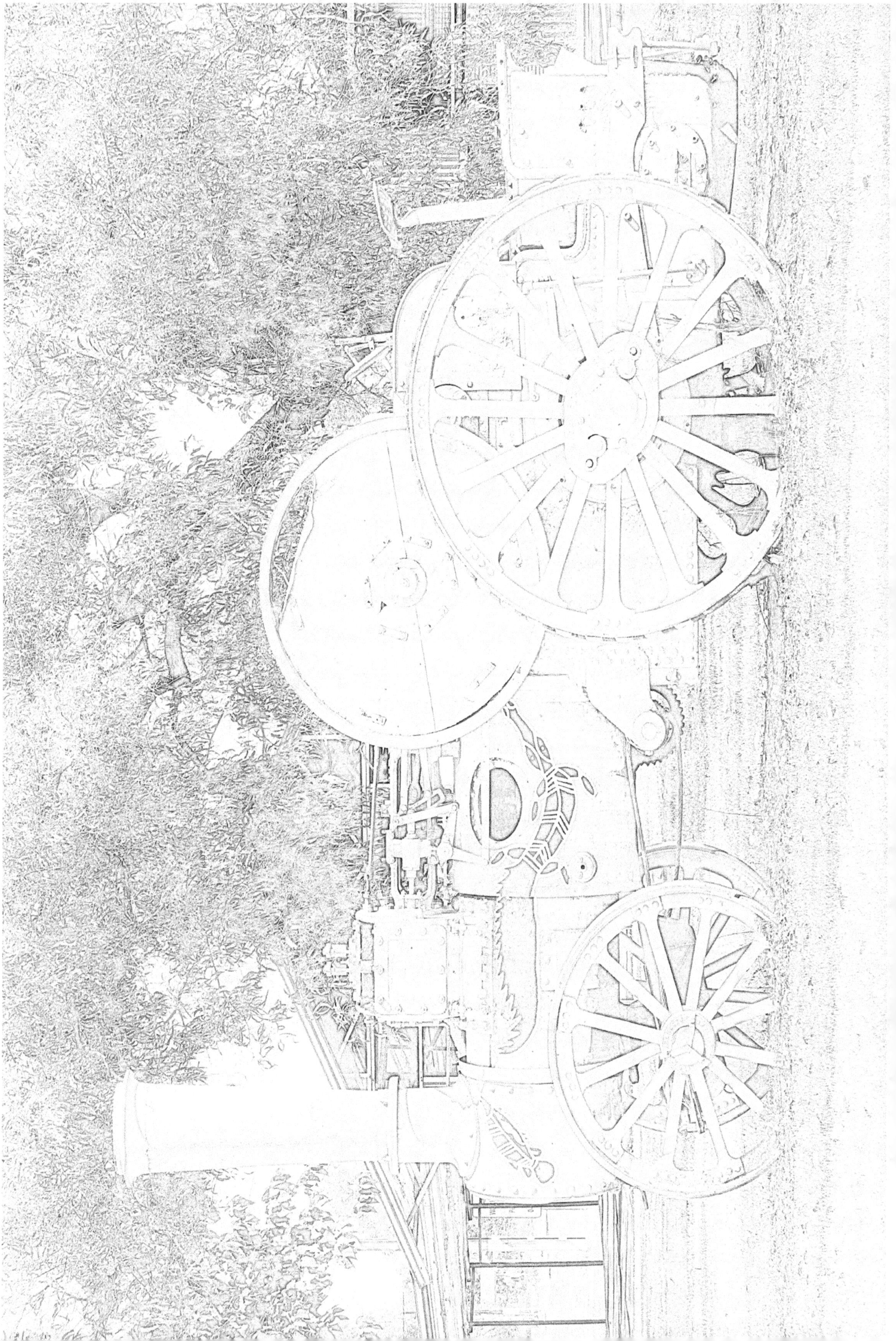

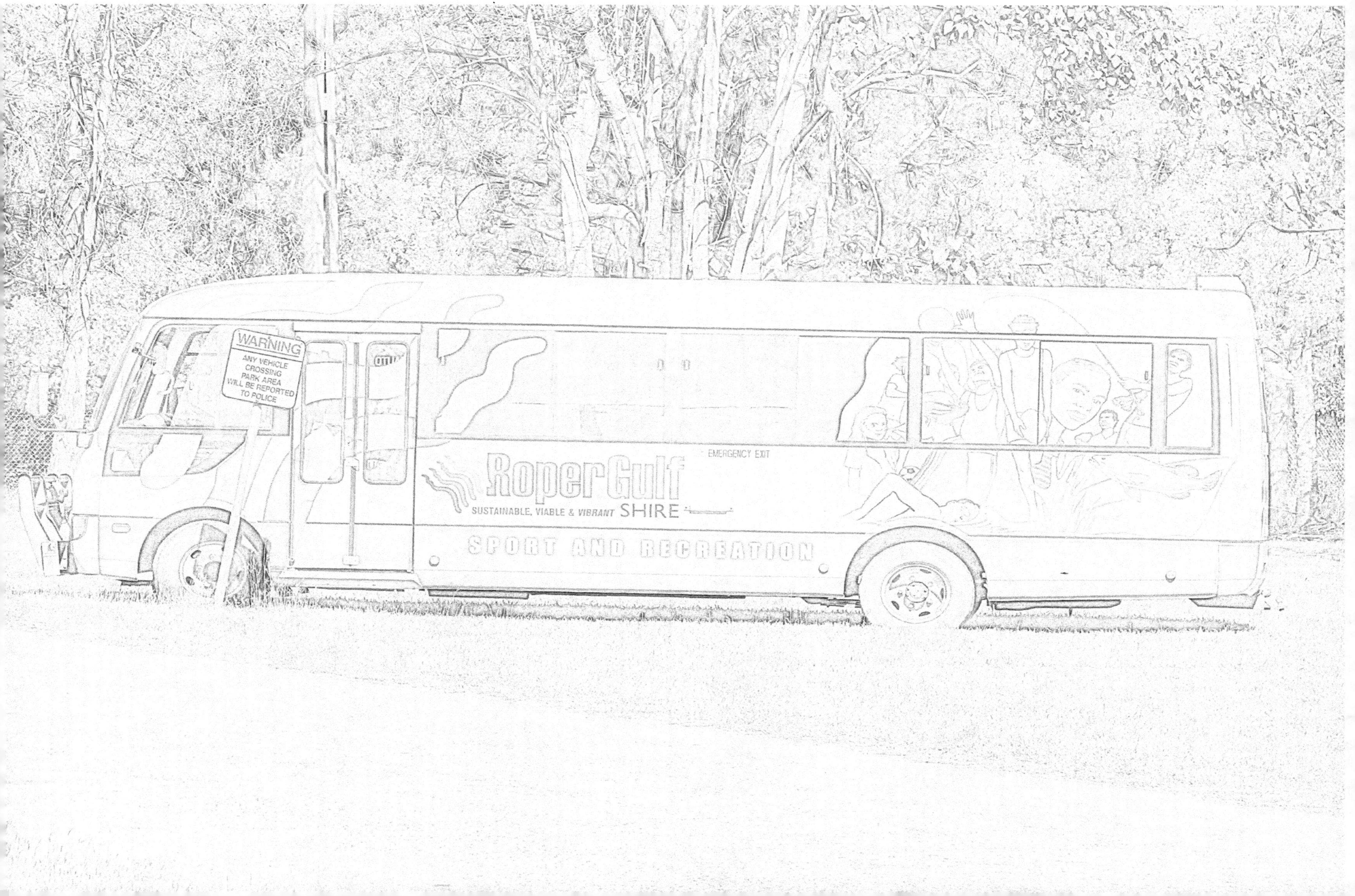
WARNING
ANY VEHICLE CROSSING PARK AREA WILL BE REPORTED TO POLICE
EMERGENCY EXIT
RoperGulf
SUSTAINABLE, VIABLE & VIBRANT SHIRE
SPORT AND RECREATION

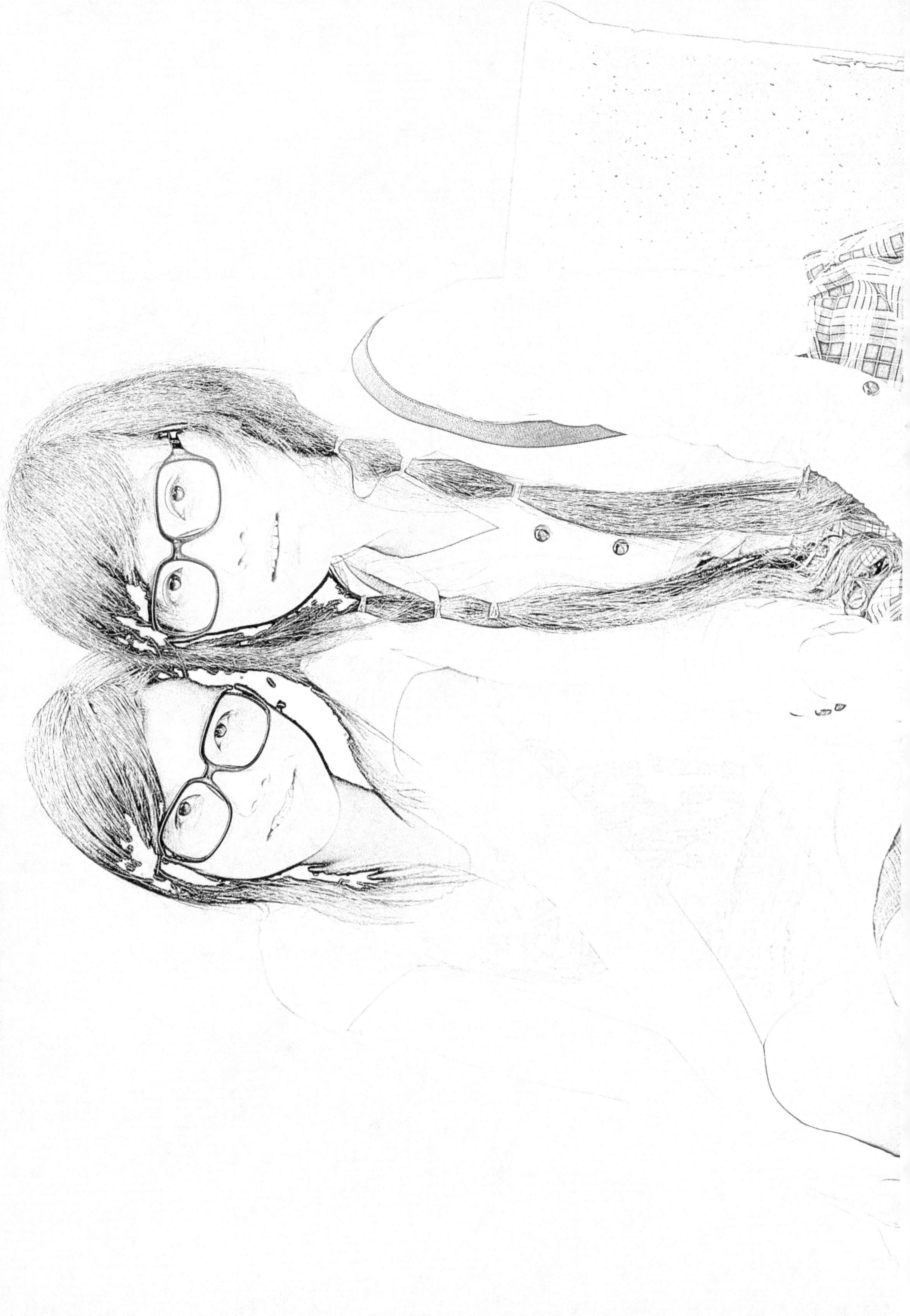

www.ingramcontent.com/pod-product-compliance
Lightning Source LLC
Chambersburg PA
CBHW081058180526
45170CB00005B/1802